A
FIELD GUIDE
TO
YOUR OWN
BACK YARD

A
FIELD GUIDE
TO
YOUR OWN
BACK YARD

John Hanson Mitchell

Illustrations by
Laurel Molk

W · W · NORTON & COMPANY
NEW YORK   LONDON

Published simultaneously in Canada by Stoddart, a subsidiary of General Publishing Co. Ltd, Don Mills, Ontario
Printed in the United States of America

The text of this book is composed in Bembo, with dispaly type set in Novarese Bold. Composition and manufacturing by The Maple-Vail Book Manufacturing Group.
Book design by Maria Epes.

FIRST EDITION

Library of Congress Cataloging in Publication Data

Mitchell, John Hanson.
   A field guide to your own back yard.

   Includes index.
   1. Urban ecology (Biology)—Northeastern States.
2. Natural history—Northeastern States.   I. Title.
QH104.5.N58M58   1985   574.974   84–14760

ISBN 0-393-01923-3

W. W. Norton & Company, Inc.
500 Fifth Avenue, New York, N.Y. 10110

W. W. Norton & Company Ltd.
37 Great Russell Street, London WC1B 3NU

1 2 3 4 5 6 7 8 9 0

for Clayton

". . . the loveliest town of all, where the houses were white and high and the elm trees were green and higher than the houses, where the front yards were wide and pleasant and the back yards were bushy and worth finding out about . . ."

E. B. White (STUART LITTLE)

CONTENTS

CONTENTS

CONTENTS

INTRODUCTION

THERE IS A POPULAR BELIEF abroad in this country that holds that the most interesting things in the natural world can only be found in faraway places or specially designated areas. That is to say, in order to experience nature you must get in your car and travel somewhere—either to a national or state park or to some official nature preserve. The nearby, that closer wilderness of the back yard and the vacant lot, is, according to the belief, entirely devoid of interesting forms of life and not worth exploring. This field guide sets out to discount that theory.

I have spent some ten to fifteen years in or near the suburbs of North America, and I think I have discovered over the years that in spite of development, in spite of our so-called technological age, the same forces and the same diversity of life that are so evident in the larger wilderness areas of the world are alive and well in the suburban back yard. A watchful eye, a little extra attention to detail, and a sharpened sensitivity to seasonal changes can uncover a veritable Serengeti Park just beyond the bedroom window. All you have to do is learn to see.

A few years ago, when I first began to get interested in outdoor subjects, I fully subscribed to the theory that one must travel in order to experience the natural world. At the time I was living not far from New York City, just over the George Washington Bridge. Regularly on weekends, or whenever I had a little extra free time, I would get in the car and drive off. I would go to the coast, to the mountains, or to some nature preserve—anywhere to escape the decidedly overdeveloped landscape of back yards and suburban streets that surrounded my house.

One of the interesting things that I discovered during these desperate jaunts into the country was the spring flight of the woodcock. The woodcock is a lowly, obscure bird with a short, chunky body and an absurdly long bill. It lives for the most part in moist woodlands and swampy areas, where it spends its life feeding on worms and similar subterranean creatures that it unearths with its sensitive, probing beak. Once a year, however, the woodcock transcends this mundane existence and rises into the sky in a magnificent nuptial flight. I used to watch them in Cornwall, Connecticut, in those early years of discovery—in early spring, just before sundown, in a low meadow by a wooded area. The first indication that there were woodcock in the area would be a low, sharp "peent" repeated over and over again. Then suddenly the peenting would stop, and if you looked carefully against the twilit sky you could see the chunky form of the woodcock burst up from a clearing and ascend higher and higher until it was out of sight. If you listened carefully you could hear its ecstatic descent. The woodcock comes back to earth in a series of barrel rolls, loop the loops, arches, twists, and turns that rival the tricks of the best stunt flyers of any air show. And all the while the air is filled with a series of pleasing whistles and chirps, created, I was to learn later, not by the woodcock's vocal cords but by the rush of wind passing through specialized feathers in its wings. The flights of the woodcock occur each year during late March or early April and are, to say the least, a fitting introduction to the season of spring.

I always used to return from my spring jaunts with a certain sense of disappointment. It seemed somehow wrong to be living in a place where there were no woodcock. Life in the suburbs of New York City seemed somehow very flat and profoundly boring. I remember in particular driving back from Connecticut one Sunday feeling the usual end of the weekend blues. It was late evening, the sun had set, and that late light of spring that even the suburbs cannot drive off was lingering in the night sky. Suddenly, from a small, undeveloped, unmowed patch of ground across the street, I heard the familiar peenting call that I had heard the evening before in Connecticut. I think I was convinced for a second that my despondency had gotten the better of me and I was cracking up. There could be no woodcock in Englewood, New Jersey, not here, a mere seven miles from Forty-second Street. But the sound persisted, and after a few seconds I heard the familiar whir of wings. I crossed the road, crept up to the little weedy patch of ground, and waited. And there, dropping out of the night sky, its ecstatic flight undiminished by its locale, was a real, live woodcock.

Since that time I have been able to find woodcock in almost any suburb within the bird's breeding range. Twice—once in Manchester, New Hampshire, and once in Boston—I found them within city limits. I have also found green frogs, spring peepers, red-backed salamanders, parula warblers, jumping mice, black walnuts, lady fern, hay-scented fern, sensitive fern, British soldier lichens, and any number of similarly obscure animals or plants generally associated with more remote or wild

INTRODUCTION

areas. Once, near Beacon Hill in the very hub of Boston, in the space of ten minutes I found five species of edible wild plants. Central Park in New York City is famous for its spring migrations. Peregrine falcons have been seen hunting around the clifflike towers of the Prudential Center in Boston, and recent surveys have found endangered species of plants or animals in the confines or the nearby suburbs of San Francisco, Savannah, Georgia, and New York City.

I don't think I have to belabor the point. I am not trying to prove that endangered species are in good shape in this country and need no further protection, and I am not suggesting that we do not need any more wildlife sanctuaries. I am simply trying to make clear the fact that a little observation can uncover a veritable Eden within walking distance of your house.

One word of caution about the book, however, or at least about the title. I have used the words *back yard* rather loosely here (not to mention the term *field guide*). The woodcock I saw in Englewood, New Jersey, was not, strictly speaking, in my own back yard. It was across the street in a lot that belonged to someone else. Many of the habitats described in the book may indeed be on your own land, but some of the best hunting areas are at the unmanaged edges of properties—the storage places behind sheds and garages, for example, the untended hedge that lines the side yard, or the no man's land between the sidewalk and the street. I do not want to encourage you to trespass, but I think it is important to explore as thoroughly as possible the apparently unowned woodlots, swamps, and wetlands. Ask permission if you have to; no one begrudges an eccentric bird watcher poking around his or her property. And even if you live in the most apparently sterile tract development, do not despair. If there is grass and a few scraggling trees, there will be wildlife. It is perhaps a hopeful sign that some of the newer suburbs—that is, those that have been constructed since the early 1970s—often have more open spaces around them than the earlier developments, and the earlier developments have had time to grow up. If you doubt my word, go off and look at Levittown, New York, the father of all suburban tracts. It has grown up and, according to friends of mine who lived there for a while, is a haven of singing birds and foraging raccoons and possums.

Woodcock

A
FIELD GUIDE
TO
YOUR OWN
BACK YARD

EARLY
SPRING

FOR A NUMBER OF YEARS NOW I have held the opinion that there are eight seasons rather than four. Anyone who has followed natural history events over any period of time will know exactly what I am talking about. There is a distinct difference between the spare, blustery landscape of late March and the lush verdure of early June, even though they both are a part of the same season. More to the point, the hot, languorous days of Indian summer are a long way from the biting snowstorms of December in spite of the fact that they both occur in fall. The natural year is in fact divided into a series of mini-seasons, each with its own weather patterns, its own hatchings or flowerings or deaths.

Of all of these eight seasons, perhaps none is more welcome than the brief season that falls between early March and mid-April. It is then that the first scents of moist earth occur, and it is then, even in the far north, that a definite change in the nature of sunlight can be sensed. This first release from the prison of winter has a way of drawing people out of doors into yards and onto porches and roof tops. You will see them there on the first warm days of March, their shirts unbuttoned for the first time since September and their faces turned upward toward the sky like those of so many pilgrims at a shrine.

EARLY SPRING

Warm sun notwithstanding, this brief interlude between the hard landscape of winter and the onset of the traditional spring is the most fickle season of the year. On one day the air may be infused with the hot light of summer, and on the very next, ranks of gray clouds may pull in from the north, bringing bitter winds and even snow. Some of the worst blizzards in the United States's history have taken place in late March, as well as some of the most tolerable, pleasant afternoons. There is only one definite thing that you can say about this season, and that is that you cannot trust it.

Nevertheless, as far as natural history is concerned, early spring is the most eventful season of the year. Everything that takes place has a sense of beginning, of veritable resurrection from the seemingly eternal death of winter. It is for this reason, undoubtedly, that more nature journals are begun at this time of year than any other. (They are ended, I should point out, sometime around mid-summer, when the year grinds to a halt that is equal only to the depth of winter.) Every event, in early spring, every shoot and bud and frog call is filled with hope of better things to come.

Spring Migrants

The return of migrating birds is an event that has some-how become thoroughly distorted in the popular mind. The robins that appear on your lawn in spring are hardly the first birds to return from the South. Even in north-ern areas, robins may spend the winter near your house if they have a decent supply of winter fruits; it's just that no one but the bird watchers and the naturalists notices them until the ground on the suburban lawns is soft enough for the robins to pluck worms from the soil.

EARLY SPRING

The other traditional sign of spring, returning swallows, actually occurs quite late in the avian spring calendar—not until May for some species, long after most of the local nesting birds have settled in.

Red-winged Blackbirds

The real harbingers of spring as far as birds are concerned are the songs of the winter residents (pp. 262–65). But even before the snow is off the ground, in some cases before the ice melts from the ponds, the true vanguard of bird migrants will arrive. Red-winged blackbirds winter south of the snow line, sometimes as far north as southern Maryland and occasionally as far north as southern New England. But if you live anywhere north of these areas, sometime in late February you may spot these handsome birds at your feeder and may be able to hear, near your yard, the familiar bubbling call that traditional field guides insist sounds like *onk-a-ree* or *o-ka-lee*.

The first redwings to come in are the few advance guard males, shiny black fellows with smashing red epaulets tinged with yellow. They will appear first in the tree tops and will drop down from time to time among the lesser beings groveling at the feeder to take sustenance before retiring again to their perches to call. As the month progresses, more and more males will arrive, followed after a few weeks by the less spectacular and less evident females. Red-wing females look like large striped sparrows.

Redwings are primarily marsh birds. Hundreds, sometimes thousands of them will stake out nest territories in some nearby wetland; a visit to a marsh any time between February and late May will be characterized partly by the racket these birds make on their nesting grounds. In contrast to some other songbird species, blackbird populations are growing in this country, and since redwings often leave the marshes to feed, you will inevitably see them passing overhead, even if you don't have a bird feeder.

Purple Grackles

Shortly after the arrival of the redwings, you may see a few purple grackles mixed in with the small flocks of male redwings. Grackles are somewhat larger than robins and have a large, wedge-shaped tail, iridescent black feathers, and fine yellow eyes. This is one of those common birds that bears close observation. Caught in the harsh light of the early spring sun, the feathers will shimmer with an array of color that can match the finest sunsets. Although he was probably mixing his ecotomes, I am certain that this is the blackbird the Hartford-based poet Wallace Stevens had in mind in "Thirteen Ways of Looking at a Blackbird."

> O thin men of Haddam,
> Why do you imagine golden birds?
> Do you not see how the blackbird
> Walks around the feet
> Of the women about you?*

Quite apart from their brilliant array of color, grackles have what seems to me, and perhaps did to Wallace Stevens as well, a particularly noble way of waddling around the lawn of your back yard. You will see them there among the robins once the grass turns green. Unlike

*From *The Collected Poems of Wallace Stevens*. Reprinted by permission of Alfred A. Knopf, Inc. Copyright 1947, 1954 by Wallace Stevens. Copyright © 1957 by Elsie Stevens and Holly Stevens.

redwings, grackles may nest in your yard, probably in a pine tree if you have one.

As with many other species of birds, evolution has equipped grackles with an invaluable method of keeping their nests clean. The droppings of the young are contained in a light, impermeable membrane known as a fecal sack. While the young are in the nest, the parents carry away the fecal sack and drop it nearby. I have discovered a number of local grackle nests simply by looking at asphalt driveways. If you see a large number of bird droppings there, even if there are no trees in the immediate area, you might look around for a grackle nest.

Other Blackbirds

Once the grackles have arrived, other blackbirds will begin to show up at your feeder or in the trees surrounding your yard. Rusty blackbirds are smaller, less colorful versions of the purple grackle. Like the redwings, they prefer wet areas, swamps as well as marshes, but they will collect with other blackbirds, such as the grackles and the redwings, and can be seen early in the spring far from water. The rusty blackbird looks a little like a redwing without the epaulet but has a pale yellow eye that stands out in sharp contrast to its shiny black feathers. The Brewer's blackbird is more common in western regions, essentially a bird of fields and prairies. Cowbirds, which are smaller still than all the other blackbirds, have a distinct coffee-brown head and neck and a peculiar bobbing, almost ducklike gait.

The cowbird has worked out an excellent, though somewhat ruthless, nesting system. Rather than build a nest of its own, the female lays her eggs in the nests of other birds while the owner is off foraging. Some species are alert to the trick and will roll the cowbird egg or eggs out of the nest. But other species, including the small yellow warbler, will proceed to incubation without a flinch. The cowbird egg hatches quickly, after some ten days or so, and the diligent victimized mother, responding to the gaping mouth of the hungry young cowbird, will feed the alien until it fledges—often at the expense of her own young. If you see these birds in your yard and expect that they may be parasitizing what you deem more favorable species, don't fret over the problem; there is nothing much you can do about it anyway. Cowbirds have been parasitizing yellow warblers and other species for millions of years, and all the species involved have so far survived.

Once the blackbird breeding season is over, many of these species remain fairly obscure for the next six weeks or so. But long before the end of summer, they will begin to collect together in roosting flocks; feeding by day in marshes, or lawns, or fields and forest, and then in the evening flying to their roosts. By late summer and early fall, these flocks can reach sizable proportions, and in the green evenings of September you can often see great rivers of blackbirds jockeying across the clearing over your back yard. It is to my mind one of the finer events of late summer.

Phoebes

Each year, around the twenty-seventh of March, I step outside in the early morning and, if the day is sunny, can hear the repeated song of the phoebe. Phoebes always seem to arrive on my land on bright mornings. The day preceding may be gray and warm, or even snowy or rainy, but on the twenty-seventh, if it is clear, the phoebe will return from its round-trip journey to southern parts of the United States.

Phoebe

It would be simple if all birds would sing their name as clearly as the phoebe. Except perhaps for the whistle-like call of the chickadee (page 263), the phoebe's call is unmistakable, and in case you don't hear it the first time, the bird will sing it again and again, seemingly without fatigue, over the next few months. The insistent call of the phoebe is one of the common sounds of an April afternoon in the back yard.

Phoebes have done well in suburbia. Formerly they would nest under cliff ledges and similarly sheltered natural spots. But with the advent of bridges and buildings, including suburban porches and garages, they have taken advantage of adversity and will plaster their nest in the most seemingly unlikely spots. One nested for two years over the screen door on my back porch.

Phoebes belong to the group of birds known as flycatchers. If you have a garden and a phoebe nest, you will see them leave some nearby perch to fly out over the garden, snap up an insect, and then retire to the perch. Although to my knowledge the phoebe is not generally recommended as a garden pest controller, undoubtedly in a single nesting season a pair of these attentive birds will consume large numbers of flying pest species. I have set up a few poles around the garden for the phoebes and the swallows to perch upon, and one of the small pleasures I have cultivated over the past few years is to lie on the couch on the back porch on spring afternoons watching the phoebes snap up cabbage moths from the broccoli patch. On still afternoons, you can even hear the sharp snap of their bills.

Tree Swallows

Approximately two weeks after the phoebes return to my yard, again on a bright and warm day, I will hear over the garden a high chirping and see the flash of white belly and blue-black wings of the tree swallow. Unlike other swallows, the tree swallows can survive fairly well in cooler weather. In some northern regions, especially along the coast, they may winter over, or at least stay in the north through December. They generally feed on insects but during autumn in the north will eat berries especially bayberries. They also seem to be highly opportunistic and, as a result, highly adaptable. On a bitterly windy October day one year I saw a huge flock of tree swallows off the south shore of Martha's Vineyard. Great blue-green combers were crashing on the beach, and about one hundred yards offshore, just above the cresting waves, there was another swirling sea of birds. The swallows had formed a huge wheel-like flock, and individual birds at the rim of the wheel were dipping down into the foam of the breaking waves. I watched them through the binoculars for a long time, but I was never able to determine whether they were feeding or simply taking in the salt water. After twenty minutes or so, the wheel stretched itself out, and the flock undulated across the beach to the moors and the bayberries.

Tree swallows nest in boxes. If you have an open yard, it is worthwhile setting up a pole with a bluebird or tree swallow box on top of it. If you are lucky enough to own a lot of land, you might set up more than one. These swallows, unlike many birds, tend to share their territories, so in theory you could generate whole flocks over your garden, thereby increasing the conscription of soldiers in your anti-garden pest army. The nests inside the boxes are lined with grasses, twigs, feathers, and strips of cloth, and when the swallows begin to nest, they avidly search out material. I always set out a few strips of rag for them. I started this practice because in their quest they were pulling apart some of the string marking my carrot rows and tearing off the little seed packets from the sticks in the garden. Tree swallows can be rather tame. There was a pair in my yard one year that would readily take strips of cloth from my out-stretched hand.

Sparrows

You may notice, with the advent of March, that there are a few new sparrows in town. The three-chirped call of the song sparrow may be one of the first signs that those sparrows that migrate are on the move, and soon after you hear the song sparrow you may be able to see the bird beneath the feeder. The heavily streaked breast with the central spot in the middle is the key field mark to watch for. However, the similarly marked and equally accomplished singer, the fox sparrow, may show up at your feeder about this time too. Fox sparrows are much larger than the average feeder sparrow and have rich fox-colored feathers. Female purple finches may also be seen at the feeder, although they may have been around all winter. Finches have fat bills, and the females have a distinct white stripe over their eyes. The tree sparrow—the bird at your feeder with the clear breast and a central dot or stickpin on its chest—and the field sparrow, with its rusty cap and pink bill, may also be more evident now, although they too will have been in the general region all winter, probably at your feeder.

Within a few weeks of the arrival of these migrant sparrows, you may be able to hear the clear, whistled call of the field sparrow. It is a series of sweet, almost elegiac notes that begins slowly enough but speeds up as the song progresses so that the end of the song is almost a continuous chirping. The song has been compared to the sound of a spinning coin or a billiard ball bounced on a table—a memorable description to my mind.

Willows

There are approximately 100 species of willow growing in the United States, some mere shrubs that bush out along slow-moving brooks, and some full-sized trees, such as the well-known weeping willow or the riverside black willow. If you have a willow in your yard, it is probably the weeping willow, originally a native of China. This may be a spindly little tree planted by a recent resident, or if your house is older, it may be a giant, all-covering thing that makes a veritable room inside its overhanging branches and sends out noxious water-seeking roots that clog your septic system lines.

No matter what the species, however, willows more or less come into their season in early spring. The long, whiplike branches of the weeping willow often offer the first glimpse of green in the winter-killed landscape, and the fuzzy catkins of the pussy willow are a favorite of schoolteachers, florists, and suburban home decorators. Pussy willows, which are a native plant, generally grow in wet areas, along stream banks, and near marshes, for example. But they will do well in dry soil as well and may be transplanted—or even planted as ornamentals in the average back yard.

If you go out gathering pussy willows in spring, you may notice that some of these small trees bear what appear to be perfect pine cones about an inch or an inch and a half in length and complete with cone-like scales. The cones are actually galls, a growth caused by a tiny fly that may emerge from the cone not long after the pussy

Willow Pine Gall

willows flower. The adult fly injects a gall-making chemical into the bud of the willow, thus forming the cone-like structure. The eggs are laid inside the gall, and the grubs may be contained in any of the cones that have not yet hatched out their adults. You can sometimes see chickadees and other birds drilling through the tops of these cones to get at the larvae inside. Cut open a few and you may find some for yourself.

Wild willows, as opposed to ornamentals such as the weeping willow, are very common in northern regions and make up a large part of the diet of many northern species of birds and mammals. Muskrats, cottontail rabbits, red and grey squirrels, meadow mice and deer all feed on the bark, buds, or foliage of the various species of willow. It is also a fairly useful plant in the human world. Apart from their ornamental value, the young branches make excellent—almost indispensable—wood for willow whistles. In fact, it is difficult for me to view these interesting plants as anything other than potential whistle material. This is the fault of a mentor from my childhood named Gilly Robinson who served as naturalist, folklorist, storyteller, hero, and entertainer for the children of the town in which I grew up.

Gilly was one of those all-around naturalists, one of a dying breed, the type of man who knows a little about almost everything in the natural world. There was no subject that didn't interest him, rocks and minerals, birds, spiders, insects, green plants, mushrooms, soil, weatherlore, Indian folktales, stars, and anything else that was in any way remotely connected with the out-of-doors. Every Saturday morning, weather permitting, he would entertain us with long nature rambles through the various woodlands around the town, all of which he knew intimately. He was a man who, in retrospect, seemed somewhere between a benevolent Pan and Santa Claus— slight of build, craggy as a rocky mountain, goat-bearded, and forever decorated in fake Indian beads, feathers, and buckskin jackets. There are not many of his type left in the average suburban town.

One of the tricks Gilly employed to get his charges to remember the wealth of detail that he imparted was to tell stories about various natural objects, and one of his favorite subjects, apart from Indian lore, was stories of ghosts, fairies, elves, brownies, and other denizens of the netherworld. He was also an accomplished craftsman, forever fashioning toys and little *objets d'art* from bits of bark or twigs or stone. Some of his finest show-pieces were the whistles he would make from willow branches.

If I remember correctly, he would slide the bark from a dried willow twig, cut a notch or sound hole at one end of the bark, and then carve out an air passage in the twig. To make the whistle, he would simply slip the bark back on the twig. We were never able to get the pure sound from our whistles that Gilly could create, but at least we learned to recognize willow trees when we saw them. I still find myself half-consciously selecting good whistle twigs whenever I am in a willow thicket.

Rainy Nights

Spring for the naturalist does not come in with flowers and bird song. Quite the contrary, it comes on dark, rainy nights filled with swirling mists, dank, froggy air, and the smell of water and earth. Long before the first flowers bloom in the woodland, a more primordial life force reasserts itself as frogs and salamanders burrow up out of the mud and earth where they have spent the winter to migrate to nearby ponds to court, mate, and lay their eggs. If you travel the roads on such nights, or even if you live in an area that is surrounded by wetlands (not an unlikely prospect in newer developments), you will notice here and there in the beam of your headlights or flashlight a low white form that looks for all the world like an animate twig or leaf. Investigate and you will find a salamander or wood frog. It is the rain that brings them out, that and some ill-understood combination of temperature, light, and perhaps yet undiscovered factors.

Once the amphibian migration has begun—and it may

begin as early as February in some latitudes—it will continue through the spring and into summer as each species, in its appointed time, migrates to the ponds to procreate. Generally the last to go are the gray tree frogs, usually sometime in mid- to late June. Once you are aware of the phenomenon of amphibian migration, you will notice that on rainy nights in the proper areas the roads may be littered with the bodies of frogs, toads, and salamanders struck down by cars as they attempt to hop, crawl, or slither across the roads from one woodland pool to the next. You must forgive them their persistent ignorance when it comes to traffic. They are cold-blooded and move slowly in cool weather, and they have been inhabiting the same basic area for some ten thousand years. The roads are the newcomers to their territory, and they have not had time to adjust.

Spotted Salamanders

Even if you refuse to go out on dank, rainy nights, some Saturday morning after the rains you may find, as you clean out your window well (or even your cellar), a glistening black creature with bright yellow spots lurking in the wet leaves at the bottom of the well. This is the yellow-spotted salamander, one of the more common

Spotted Salamander

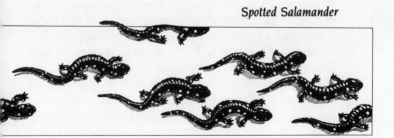

amphibians in the eastern United States. Recent studies have indicated that the biomass of salamanders in a given woodland may outweigh that of birds, and yet, for all their numbers, spotted salamanders are rarely seen.

For eleven and a half months of the year they live in damp holes in burrows feeding on worms and other invertebrates. Once a year, on the first wet nights of spring, they will desert their holes to migrate to small temporary ponds in the woods. After mating, the female lays a clutch of some 200 eggs encased in a clear jellylike substance. In two to four weeks the eggs will hatch and the larvae will emerge. The larvae of the spotted salamander, and for that matter of most salamanders, look exactly like frog tadpoles except that they have tiny branchlike appendages behind their heads that serve as gills. Before spring is over, the larvae will develop into adults and leave the temporary ponds to take up life in the underground. Long since, their parents will have returned to their customary hole to spend the next year. If it survives the migration, the yellow-spotted salamander may live to ten or eleven years of age—a mere six months of which will be spent above ground.

Jefferson's Salamanders

If you visit the ponds where the spotted salamanders congregate, you may also find there an animal that looks a little like a spotted salamander without its spots. The Jefferson's salamander is five to seven inches long, ranges in color from dark brown to an almost blue black, and is speckled or dappled with flecks of delicate blue. Like the spotted salamanders, these handsome amphibians spend eleven months of the year in burrows or tunnels in the soil. They feed on subterranean invertebrates, and even though some of them may dwell as much as four feet beneath the surface, the message of spring somehow penetrates to their underground world. On those magical rainy nights in early spring, often accompanied by spotted salamanders, wood frogs, and spring peepers, they will head for the temporary ponds to mate and lay their eggs.

Salamander mating rituals involve a great deal of thrashing and wriggling, after which the males and the females pair off, mating is accomplished, and several clusters of egg masses containing as many as forty eggs will be laid. Within a month or so—although the period may be longer if the conditions are not right—the eggs will hatch and the larval salamanders will remain in the pond for the next three months.

As with the spotted salamander and the wood frog (pp. 270–73), periodically during the annual migrations some of these migrants may end up in your cellar. You may also find them under leaves or mulch in your garden. I once found a handsome Jefferson's salamander sitting in the middle of an asphalt driveway on a rainy April morning, and I have also seen them at night in the parking lots under street lights. The best place to see them, however, is on rainy, wet roads in rural areas with a lot of swamps. Pick your night well and you are bound to turn up something.

Unfortunately, both the Jefferson's, the related bluespotted, and the yellow-spotted are becoming rare, the victims of acid precipitation. The high acidity of the waters of their breeding ponds, caused by the runoff from acidic snows, prevents the embryos of these salamanders from developing; they die before they even get a chance to be born. I have visited known breeding ponds that were empty of salamanders which ten years earlier contained as many as 200 thrashing individuals.

Red-backed Salamanders

There is another salamander that may appear in your basement during the wet months of early spring. The red-backed or lead-backed salamander is not as spectacular as its more flamboyant cousin, but it makes up in numbers what it lacks in color. Red-backs are very common and can be seen pretty much throughout the year. You can often find them in summer under rocks and inside rotting logs, or even in the damp logs at the bottom of your woodpile. They may appear again in your cellar in autumn, and I have even found them during the winter under rocks in running water.

As the name implies, redbacks are characterized, in many individuals at least, by an overall reddish color. The red ones often have a wide stripe running down their backs that may be yellow, light red, or even pink and is often edged by black. Generally, though, the appearance of the redback is a dull, nondescript red—or black, or gray, or, it seems, anything in between. Size may be the key identifying characteristic. They are small salamanders, no more than three and a half inches usually, and relatively slender. If you find a small, skinny salamander in your cellar, chances are it is a red-backed.

This is probably one of the more common salamanders in suburban areas, since it can endure fairly dry conditions and will seek a hideout in almost any convenient shelter, including old boards and debris in inner-city areas. I once found one under a Frisbee that had been lost in the grass in a school yard some seasons earlier.

The redback is the "lizard" that is often discovered by schoolchildren, and according to youthful reports, it is a dangerous animal with a poisonous tongue, a poisonous bite, a stinger on its tail, and a number of similar legendary variations. One wonders what legends would emerge had these children known that the redback and a few other salamanders are equipped with row upon row of teeth, including teeth on the roof of the mouth.

Salamanders are *not* lizards. There is one golden rule to help you distinguish the two; if you can catch it, it is a salamander, if you can't, it is a lizard (pp. 120–22).

Tiger Salamanders

There are many other species of salamanders, but generally these interesting amphibians have a relatively limited range; they are found mostly in the mid-Atlantic states and the Northeast. Of all the species, however, the one with the greatest range and perhaps the most common salamander in the United States is the tiger salamander. It is also among the more colorful—highly patterned in yellow and black, although the coloration may vary from individual to individual. It can be found in a wide range of habitats, everything from arid plains to high-elevation forests.

The tiger salamander is fairly large. Females—the larger of the sexes—may grow to ten inches, although eight inches is more common. Like its relative, the spotted salamander, it mates in the spring—somewhat earlier, in fact, within its range than the spotted. The kidney-shaped eggs are laid in shallow waters, and most of the aquatic larvae leave the ponds upon reaching adulthood. However, although you won't find them in your yard unless you have a pond, some tiger salamanders never grow up. The adults simply retain the larval gills that permit them to breathe underwater and spend the rest of their lives in the ponds where they were born. Partly because of this curious extended childhood, and partly because tiger salamanders are common and easy to catch, they are a favorite of collectors for biological supply houses. Many high-school biology students may be familiar with this amphibian, not because they have seen it in their back yards or neighborhood ponds but because they have dissected it on lab tables.

Collecting salamanders for biological supply houses is an odd way to pick up a few bucks, but apparently the custom is common enough to threaten local populations, especially of the acid rain-endangered yellow-spotted salamander. A friend of mine who studies these things told me that the collectors do their work in early spring during the mating season. As a student of salamanders, he is an habitué of remote ponds in deeply wooded areas in rural sections of the East. He says that even on the darkest, rainiest nights in the most desolate, trackless forests he has encountered soggy collectors emerging from the gloom, carrying burlap bags filled with as many as 150 squirming tiger salamanders.

Froggy Nights

There is a little bit of German folklore that holds that frogs are spontaneously generated by heavy rains in spring. Needless to say, perhaps, frogs are hatched from eggs that are laid in water; they develop into tadpoles and then undergo a metamorphosis that rivals any folklore for fantastical transformations. Nevertheless, on rainy nights in early spring one can understand how the folklore developed. You have but to drive the back roads of any reasonably well-watered region on such a night to see the hopping forms of hundreds of frogs crossing the road. Furthermore, on a good rainy night you can sometimes find frogs and toads in your own back yard, and very often you can hear them calling.

Perhaps the most famous caller of the spring night is

Spring Peeper

the tiny frog known as the spring peeper. The song of this frog, a bell-like sound or sharp, whistled "peep," can carry as much as a mile if the atmospheric conditions are right. If you live within the range of the spring peeper and there are unpolluted wetlands in your area, you should be able to hear the peeper chorus. If you step outdoors some rainy night in April and hear the sound of distant jingle bells, you are hearing the mating call of these small frogs.

Sometimes you can find spring peepers in your house, especially in the cellar. They are surprisingly small for so loud a creature, no more than an inch or two long, and they have a characteristic **X** mark on their backs. Generally they are brown in color, but some range from pale brown to green or even gray. The peeper chorus will continue through March and April and into May in most parts of its range. The idea of the chorus, the idea of all frog calls, in fact, is to attract the females. After mating the female spring peeper lays anywhere from 700 to 1,000 eggs, either individually or sometimes in small clusters of about ten. The eggs are encased in a jellylike substance, and if you find any, you can often see the developing tadpole inside the clear jelly—something that is true of other frogs and salamander eggs as well. The eggs will hatch in a week or two, depending upon the weather conditions and the temperature of the water. The tadpoles will remain in the water for about three months, feeding on aquatic vegetation. Once metamorphosis takes place, the frogs climb out of the water and disperse to the surrounding territory.

It is interesting that although a great deal is known about the mating habits of this common frog, not much is known about the other nine months of its life. Spring peepers are tree frogs—you can see the tiny pads on the ends of their toes that assist them in climbing—and it is known that they feed on other animals, primarily flies, mosquitoes, gnats, and beetles. But where they go to do their feeding, where and how they spend the winter, is not known.

Theirs is perhaps the most commonly heard frog call in the East. I came north from Florida in a decidedly slow-motion trip one year and was within hearing of spring peeper calls from January to July. They called from roadside ditches, from deep within cypress swamps, from culverts along the New Jersey Turnpike, and from the spruce-studded shores of northern ponds in Maine. Furthermore, the singular call of this frog can be heard in almost any month of the year.

Toads

The call of the wood frog (see page 272), coming as it does after the long silence of winter, is a welcome sound in the landscape. And the great ringing chorus of spring peepers, the traditional harbinger of spring, is a clarion call that announces that although there may yet be a few cold days, the winter is over. But to my mind, the most beautiful amphibian call of spring is sung by what is traditionally one of the "uglies" of folklore and fantasy tales—the poor, maligned toad. Sometime in April, about the time that the grass turns green on your lawn, you may hear some warm night a long, drawn-out trill that starts from a low note, rises quickly in pitch, and then sustains itself for half a minute or so. The song has a distinct flutelike quality and, half-heard through the mists of a warm April evening, carries with it all the rich sense of rebirth and regeneration associated with spring.

The animal that makes this beautiful call hardly needs description. Ugly though they are thought to be, they are often the subject of posters, cards, and cartoons—

not to mention illustrated books of fairy tales. Toads seem to prefer shallow waters for mating; they will sometimes lay their eggs in a mere puddle, although in dry years this can be disastrous for the young tadpoles. The eggs are easy to recognize: they are contained in long, gelatinous strings that may hold as many as six or seven thousand eggs. The tadpoles hatch quickly, less than two weeks after the eggs are laid, generally, and they will metamorphose into adults in about six to eight weeks. The young toads are tiny versions of the adults, no longer than the nail of your little finger. If you see one of them, be sure to look for more; they tend to leave their birth ponds *en masse* in my experience. On several occasions I have come across veritable packs of them hopping through the forests as if engaged in some secret invasion.

Although I'm sure this is a poor ecological practice, for a while I was in the habit of catching the toads I would find on my woods walks and bringing them home to the garden. Toads, along with praying mantises and a few other predators, are among the gardener's best friends. It has been estimated that a single toad in a garden will consume more than 200 insects in a night, most of them pest species. (It is also true, however, that toads will consume useful species—earthworms, spiders, other predatory insects—but such is the price of organic pest control.)

Even if you don't live near water, it is likely that toads will appear in your garden or yard at some point during the summer. They are primarily nocturnal animals and spend most of the day buried in the ground or under cool logs or burrowed beneath rocks. But when evening comes, they emerge to scour the lawn and garden for food. Since insects tend to be attracted to patio lights and other outdoor lighting systems, you can often find toads there as well.

Toads do not give you warts, but the copious amount of liquid they release whenever you try to pick them up is toxic to some extent and will irritate the inside of the mouths of curious dogs, cats, and other, more serious toad predators. That other common night prowler of the suburbs, the skunk, often feeds on toads. Skunks will play with a toad or roll it in soil, forcing it to expell its supply of toxic urine. The hognosed snake that may appear in your back yard during the summer months can also feed on toads with impunity; the toad is its prime source of food, in fact.

SPRING

I HAVE COME to believe that the onset of spring was a far more important event before the invention of radio and television. For one thing people—children and adults alike—were not half so sated as they are now with exciting news and entertainments. As a result, the greening of the fields, or the opening of the first flower in the dooryard gardens or in the nearby woodlands, must have assumed great importance. You have but to peruse some of the turn-of-the-century nature guides or journals in order to get a sense of what I mean. They are filled with data on the first blossoming of wildflowers, the first arrivals of birds, and the first appearance of a woodchuck. It is fairly safe to assume that the average exurban kid in the nineteenth century knew more about the wildflowers and the birds of his or her neighborhood than the average suburban adult of today knows about the flowers in the back yard.

In spite of the environmental degradation that has taken place since the turn of the century, the natural world, even in overused suburban areas, hasn't changed so drastically as to prevent discovery of some of the small adventures that inspired the journals of the nineteenth-century door-yard explorers. What seems to have changed is the human mind. Nevertheless, the talent for obser-

SPRING

vation is a learned art, and with very little effort it is possible within a single year to become intimate with the natural environment of your immediate neighborhood. The best place to begin, of course, is your own back yard.

The spring that was so carefully documented in the journals of nineteenth-century naturalists is without question the most celebrated event in the natural world, even today. In a sense, spring actually begins in February with the hooting of the great horned owls and other less-observed events. But sometime in April or in May in the far north, the air will warm, the grass will turn green, and the glory of spring will descend. To my mind, although they are charged with meaning and promise, the small springtime events of February and March cannot compare with the real thing. There is no day in all the year that can match a May morning in the garden with the air soft, the great chorus of songsters filling the landscape, the smell of fresh-turned earth, the scent of apple blossoms, and a clear, bright sky. This is the long-awaited season when it is neither too hot nor too cold, when all the world is right and all complaints about the weather are rendered meaningless.

Woodland Wildflowers

There is a brief period in spring between the time that the weather warms up and the trees go into leaf when the woodland floor becomes a floral arrangement that blossoms with a variety of colors and delightful odors. Many herbaceous woodland plants are in deep shade most of the year, but in response to the length of day, the temperature, the light, and no doubt a number of yet undetermined factors, some of the best-known wildflowers go into bloom. Unfortunately, partly as a result of the hunter-gatherer mentality of nineteenth-century nature lovers and partly because farmers regularly turned their cows loose in open woodlands, some of the more beautiful of these subtle flowers have become somewhat rare. But no matter how few, they generally offer the first dash of color after the sere landscape of winter and as a result are very much a part of the floral folklore of poets and nature writers.

Whether you will be able to find any of these delights in your back yard depends on the nature of the landscape that existed in the area before your house was put there. If you are lucky enough to have a wooded yard—what the developers and real-estate agents like to term "a naturally landscaped property"—you may find a few. If you live in former farmland or prairie, you may have to wait until later in the spring. But sometime between March and April, if you have trees on your property, be sure to check the leaf litter and the hidden corners for the small, often obscure blossoms that will appear there once the weather warms up.

Trailing Arbutus

One of the classic victims of the over-zealous nature of wildflower gatherers is the trailing arbutus. This plant, also known as mayflower, is one of the more popular ornaments of the literature of early spring and, in season, used to be hawked on the streets of Boston and other New England cities. It is by tradition the first to go into blosom; there are reports of arbutus blooming *beneath* the snow cover of the March woods. Whether this is true or not probably depends more on the fickle climate than the blooming date. I have never found the flower before April in New England, although it is such an obscure little plant I probably miss a lot of blossoms.

Arbutus has a running stem set with rounded ever-green leaves that are covered with rusty hairs. The flowers, which are like small tubes with flaring tops, are generally pink. They have a delicious aroma, perhaps the first scent to fill the air since the demise of the goldenrods in the previous autumn. For this reason, and probably because of its early blossoming date, it was a favorite of nineteenth-century nature poets—"the flowers of God," one poet called them.

Hepatica

Hepatica is another one of the early bloomers and another one of the flowers that was beloved in the nineteenth century. The blossoms are generally lilac-colored, although they can vary from almost white to pink, and the leaves are rounded and thick and have three lobes. Another name for this plant is liver leaf, and it is probable that the flower fell victim to the ancient doctrine of signatures, which holds that the shape of a plant determines its pharmacological use. Hepatica is Greek for liver, and it may have been considered a tonic for liver ailments at some point. The doctrine of signatures reflects another view of the world—still prevalent in the nineteenth century—that God had ordered the world according to human needs.

Toothwort

Another wildflower to watch for in spring if there is wooded land near your house is the toothwort. There are a number of species in this genus, but the most widespread is the cut-leaf toothwort, which has a flower with four petals bunched together in a cluster at the end of a stem. The leaves of the flower are arranged around the stem of the plant in a whorl, and each leaf is divided into three sections so that unless you look carefully you would say there are nine leaves instead of three. The flowers are usually whitish or pale purple. Look for variations of the toothwort throughout the United States.

The roots of these plants are long and fleshy, reaching in some cases as much as a foot into the ground. If you find one toothwort on your land, you are likely to find any number, so you might pull one or two up, wash the root, and taste it. This is one of the many plants in the mustard family, and the root has a characteristic peppery taste, a flavor vaguely resembling watercress. It is a favorite among wild-food gourmets; in the days when there were more woods and more good stands of toothwort, it made a convenient condiment for woodland forays and picnics.

Bloodroot

Bloodroot is another plant with an interesting rootstock. The plant grows from about five to ten inches high, has a beautiful white flower with eight ot ten petals, and rounded, lobed leaves. Bloodroot first pierces through the leaf litter of the forest floor as a spearpoint or a narrow cigarillo. The bud of the flower is wrapped tightly in the leaves and opens after the leaves unfurl and extend themselves.

If you dig up bloodroot and break open the large, fleshy root, or if you break the stem by the base, the plant will exude a red juice. Since the root is large and vaguely resembles the roots of toothwort and other edible tubers, bloodroot is sometimes eaten by mistake. It is, fortunately, not very good eating; even the smallest quantity has a bitter, acidic taste that discourages people from finishing their wild repast; consumed in large amounts it is believed to be poisonous. Bloodroot is a

Bloodroot

truly beautiful flower, and blooming as it does on the heels of a colorless winter, it is best left growing where it is. Consider yourself fortunate if you find it on your land.

Field Flowers

Somewhat later in the spring, after the leaves come out on the trees and the weather has warmed, the wildflowers that bloom in open areas, including a few unwanted plants on your lawn, will come into blossom. Some of these are categorized as weeds by ardent guardians of the green lawn, but others, such as the wild geranium and the bluet, are more commonly found in rougher old field-type habitats that have not been assiduously mowed once a week. These flowers have a beauty that is equal or superior even to the woodland wildflowers, and yet, since they come later in the season, when everything, including the ornamental garden plants, has gone into flower, they do not receive half the praise or credit that is given to their earlier-blooming compatriots. Nevertheless, if you have a section of your land that you are willing to leave unmowed, watch for these sometime in May or April.

Wild Geranium

Wild geranium may appear in a forgotten corner of your yard if you have a lot of trees. They are wildflowers of open woodlands and shaded roadsides, and although they will also grow in open fields, they will often move into the shaded setting of the treed suburban lot. These are no relation to the potted geraniums that are sold in nurseries. The name comes from the Greek word for crane, which is a reference to the beaklike appearance of the fruits of these flowers; another name for wild geranium is the cranesbill. Allow a few to go to seed on your property and you will see the logic of the name. The leaves of this plant are divided into five lobed parts, the flowers a pale red or pink and rather large for a wildflower. Some have been domesticated and are sold in nurseries as ornamentals.

Bluets, or Quaker Ladies

If you have moved onto property that has poor soil, or if there is a vacant lot or meadow near you, sometime in April, often before the other field wildflowers go into bloom, you may notice that a whole section of the land will go into color as if the ground had been carefully landscaped. Look more carefully and you will see that the mat of color is created by tiny blue and white flow-

Quaker Ladies

ers centered with a bright yellow eye. Bluets, or Quaker Ladies, as they are also called, do well in poor soils, and in fact the color may be a reflection of the acidity of the soils in the general area. They often form large mats, in some cases crowding out other plants. But the rank beds of color and the delicacy and beauty of the flowers themselves far outweigh any damage or nuisance these flowers may cause.

Violets

There are nearly 100 species of violets found in the United States and Canada, many of them common and often unwanted residents of moist suburban lawns. They have heartshaped leaves and five-petaled flowers, which generally appear on a separate stalk. Some violets have a spur or horn-shaped appendage just behind the petals. Many species have been domesticated and are sold as house plants or garden flowers, but the wild ones, the surprises, so to speak, of the back yard, are to my mind the more beautiful, although they are decidedly smaller.

Not all violets are bluish in color. In your own yard you may be able to find the yellow violet, the white, and various shades of purple to blue. If you look carefully at the violets in your yard, you may notice that lower down on the stem there are less conspicuous flowers that appear to have failed to open. These are technically known as cleistogamous flowers, which means they are self-fertilizing. The seeds will ripen inside the flowers without the benefit of cross-fertilization. This little bit of insurance is no doubt part of the reason that violets have done so well in the world. As any gardener who has brought them into his or her yard will testify, violets have a way of escaping from their beds and reappearing in places where they are not expected.

SPRING

Violet flowers are edible. They are sometimes sugared and sold as candies, and they can also be made into syrups and jellies, but I have found that the best violets are the raw ones. Simply scoop up a few while you are sitting on the lawn some spring afternoon. They have a distinct violet taste—very fresh and very springlike. Don't worry about eating them all up. Violets are prolific, and in any case, the real seed producers are the unopened flowers low on the stems.

Buttercups

There are about thirty-six species of buttercups in North America, but one of them, the bulbous buttercup, has done pretty well for itself on suburban lawns. Like all buttercups, it has shiny yellow flowers shaped like perfect little cups, and leaves that are segmented and deeply lobed. This is one of those common plants that has managed to enter the folklore of rural America. Lovesick country swains would pluck a flower and hold it under the chin of their beloved; if the yellow of the flower reflected up on her chin, she was presumed to be in love. This is one of those fail-safe tests that often appear in folklore. Since the petals of the buttercup are shiny, almost varnished to brightness, they always reflect yellow on the chin. Try the test for yourself even if you aren't in love. If you are cynical about matters of love, I heard from my children a more prosaic use of the buttercup. If the yellow appears, they say it proves you love butter.

The American Indians had a more practical use for the buttercup. They would boil the roots and eat them, and they used to make a flour from the parched seeds and would use the juice of the plant as a yellow dye.

Dandelion

Of all the common weeds that grow on the average suburban lawn, perhaps none is more despised or more
enduring than the dandelion. This native of Eurasia is
now common throughout the United States and Canada. It grows not only on lawns but between sidewalk
cracks, along railroad lines, on city streets, in parks, and
almost anyplace that has enough sunlight. If you can
overlook your prejudice, or if you can manage to give
up any devotion you may harbor for the smooth, albeit
sterile, greensward of the American lawn, the dandelion
emerges as one of the more interesting weeds in all of
America.

For one thing, at least in my view, it is a classy and
very colorful flower, all the more so when a group of
them get together and make a bright yellow carpet on
the green spring fields. It also tends to flower late in the
season and is often the last plant to flower in my yard in
late November. What is more, when it goes to seed it
forms a beautiful rounded seedhead consisting of tiny
parachutelike bits of fluff, each with its passenger of seed.
Blowing the seeds from the flowerhead still brings delight
even to the jaded TV-addicted children of our time; you
have but to send a pack of them out into a field of dandelions in seed to prove it. Furthermore, the dandelion
leaves make a delicious potherb early in the spring before
the plants go into flower.

On my way to work I drive past a large hayfield near
the Sudbury River in Concord, Massachusetts. As regularly as the return of the phoebes, in late April in that
field I used to see loose groups of older women and men
with baskets, picking something amidst the young shoots
of grass. I stopped to find out what they were doing one
year and, using my broken but adequate Italian, learned

that they had come out from the North End—the Italian district—in Boston and were picking dandelion greens for salads and potherbs. They very proudly offered the raw leaves to me, and, munching the slightly bitter but fresh-tasting breakfast, we stood there for a while kissing our fingers in delight, gesturing at the beauty of the fields, the beauty of the river, the beauty of the spring day, and the delicious taste of our dandelion greens. I have stopped there each spring ever since.

It is also possible to make a palatable wine from the flowers of the dandelion. A friend of mine on Martha's Vineyard used to make gallons of it each summer and spend the winters' "sipping summer with dinner," as he put it. This noxious weed also has some commercial value. As late as the 1950s hundreds of thousands of pounds of the roots were imported into the United States for medicinal purposes.

Spring Butterflies

Once the flowers have blossomed in your garden, once the grass has turned green and the young plants of the garden have leafed out, you will begin to see, even in heavily built-up suburbs, what Robert Frost referred to as "flying flowers"—namely, butterflies. To every butterfly there is a season. Like flowers, they emerge at certain times of the year, according to what their food plants are doing at the time. Each of these beautiful insects depends on a certain plant or group of plants as a food source, and if you happen to have some of these plants in your yard, and in some cases even if you don't, you will undoubtedly see them from time to time fluttering across the lawn.

Spring Azures

Butterflies are traditionally creatures of bright sun and languid summer days, but there are a few species that more or less specialize in spring, some of which appear quite early in the year. Most famous among these is the mourning cloak (pp. 273–74), but sometimes even before the frosts have disappeared you may spot a tiny bright blue butterfly known as the spring azure. The spring azure has one of the widest ranges of any butterfly in North America. It can be found from Florida to Alaska and, since there are several hatchings, can be spotted in your yard throughout the warmer seasons. It hatches in early spring from a chrysalis formed by a larva back in the autumn, although in more southerly regions you can see this butterfly even in winter. The larvae look a little like small slugs and hardly match the splendor of the colorful adults.

If you have dogwoods on your land, you may be able to see the feeding larvae. You may also notice that clustered around the larvae are a number of black ants. The ants are more or less the cowherds of these innocent grazers. Periodically you will see an ant touch a larva with its antennae, thereby causing the larva to release a sweet fluid that the ants feed upon. This appears to be a common adaptation among ants; they also feed on honeydew excreted by certain species of aphids.

Cabbage Butterflies

By the time the broccoli in your garden is headed up, you may notice, fluttering over the cabbage patch, a white butterfly with black spots on the upper side of its wings. Experienced gardeners may sense a sinking feeling seeing these delicate flyers, for they are the only butterfly that is a serious pest on crops. The fat green larvae of the cabbage butterfly feed voraciously on plants in the cabbage family, often burrowing into the heads of broccoli or deep within a cabbage head in their quest for food. If you are an organic gardener, or if you don't clean your vegetables thoroughly after harvesting them from the garden, you may turn up a few of these in the cooking pot or even on the dinner plate. Not to be alarmed. A friend of mine who is a wild-food enthusiast used to purposely allow the caterpillars to remain in some of his more exotic Chinese mixed vegetable dishes. He had the nasty habit of serving delicious meals and informing his guests *after* dinner of the contents of the dish.

Tiger Swallowtails

By May the beautiful tiger swallowtail butterflies will emerge from their overwintering pupae. They are large butterflies, about five inches across, and are handsomely marked with a strong tiger pattern—black stripes on a yellow background. These butterflies also have elongated hind wings that end in tails, not unlike the tail of a barn swallow. The caterpillars feed on basswood, willow, birch, and poplar, any of which may be found in your back yard. Once you see the larva of this butterfly, you will not be likely to forget it. The caterpillar is about two inches long when it is mature and appears to have two great glaring eyes on its head. These are mere eyespots, a mimic feature designed to frighten off predators. The real eyes, as you will see if you look carefully, are on the head of the caterpillar, where all good eyes should be, not in the back. If you dare to touch this hideous glaring worm, it will shoot out two toxic-looking orange "horns." Leave it alone and the horns will withdraw. Touch it again and they will sprout. The horns

Tiger Swallowtail Butterfly

are not dangerous, but one presumes that if the huge eyes fail to scare off predators, the horns will finish the work.

Black Swallowtails

The related black swallowtail is slightly smaller than the tiger swallowtail and generally holds its wings erect after it lands. The edges of the black wings are marked with

SPRING

a double border of yellow spots on the forewings. The hind wings have a flashing of blue inside the yellow spots and have a bright orange patch at the base. Like its relatives, this butterfly has the characteristic swallow tails. The adults emerge in May. A few weeks after you see the butterflies you may find a handsomely ringed green caterpillar munching contentedly on your favorite parsley plants. Beautiful as this butterfly is, its voracious larvae can do in a good row of carrots or strip an entire parsley plant in an afternoon. Since this butterfly is rarely abundant (unlike the cabbage butterfly), one of the easiest controls is to simply hand-pick the caterpillars. You may notice a strong carrotlike odor when you handle them—yet another weapon in the caterpillar defense arsenal. If you have children, you might keep one of these caterpillars in a jar with a screened top. Feed it carrot tops or parsley leaves. The caterpillar will pupate, and before the end of summer a handsome adult will emerge in the jar.

Morels

The majority of mushrooms that you will find in the confines of your back yard fruit from late summer through the first frosts. But there is one group, the morels, that generally appear in spring and that are counted among the most delectable of all the mushrooms that grow in the New World. Morels are easy to recognize; for one thing, there aren't many other mushrooms that grow at this time of year, and furthermore, they have distinct pitted brown caps that look like very few other mushrooms, except the so-called false morel.

There is a morel cult that exists among the more esoteric naturalists who live within the range of this mushroom. The general belief among these cultists holds that

Morel

morels are more or less unpredictable mushrooms that are hard to find. As a result, the location of a good morel patch is often a closely guarded secret among mushroom fanciers. Morels tend to favor old orchards and, according to some mushroom guides, burnt-over areas. But I have found them growing in several of the back yards I have inhabited; one patch grew right by the steps of a front porch. I also found a good bunch growing under a privet bush on the main street of Concord, Massachusetts, and I have found them growing in friends' yards in the Berkshires. They do seem to be erratic, however. They tend to appear in one year and then never fruit again, it seems.

I learned the prime lesson of mushroom gathering one

year from a group of morels. I was scything down a clump of American bamboo and uncovered a large patch of these delicious mushrooms. There are several species of morels, all of which are edible, and I proceeded to collect them, intent on a good lunch of morels on buttered toast with poached eggs. The mushrooms I had found had all the classic morel field marks—pitted caps, brown coloration, and clear white stems, but the caps were irregular, not conical. I had heard of false morels and knew them to be toxic, but since I had never seen any in all my years of mushroom hunting, I assumed these were safe. I knew that you should never eat any mushroom unless you have positively identified it, but I had left all my mushroom field guides at a friend's house, so I couldn't check them. I debated for a while after I collected my morels, left then on the kitchen table, got involved in more scything, and then decided not to chance it and put the morels in the refrigerator until the following Monday. As you can guess, they turned out to be false morels, which, although they won't kill you, can make you decidedly ill.

Spring Fungi

There are a few other fungi that may appear in spring. If you have any rotting wood in your yard, or if you keep a pile of wood chips, or even if you mulch with wood chips, you may notice after an extended period of wet weather a brightly colored jellylike substance clinging to the wood chips or the wood of the log. These are probably the aptly named jelly fungi, which can appear sometimes even in winter after the snow has melted and the wood the fungi grows on has received a good soaking. Some of these have rather prosaic common names, such as yellow jelly fungus or white jelly fungus, but there is a common species that always brings to mind my old nature mentor, Gilly Robinson.

One of his favorite fungi was a small yellow growth that would appear on stumps and logs in the woods Gilly led us through. "Here," he would say whenever he would come across it. "Here is where the witches had their sandwiches last night. Do you see? One of them dropped her butter." Never mind that the common name for this fungi is witch's butter and that he probably made up the story to fit the name; I am able to recognize this species whenever I come across it. Witch's butter may appear in your back yard, generally on the wood chip mulch after a period of rain in almost any season.

Several other fungi may appear as well. Among these is a group that Gilly would refer to as "smokers." Gilly's smokers are tiny, cup-shaped fungi, often brightly colored, which, quite fittingly, go by the common name of cup fungi. There are many species, but they have one abiding characteristic that is the delight of small children. If you breathe on them, the moist, warm air of your breath will cause them to send out their spores in tiny, smokelike clouds. I have forgotten the little bit of folklore that Gilly made up to account for this phenomenon—there is no doubt in my mind that he had a legend for it—but true to form, I have not forgotten the fungus itself. I can still remember the excitement he would express every time he found a smoker. He would crouch over, snatch it up, tell us to watch carefully, breathe on it, and marvel with the rest of us at the mystic smoke that emerged from the tiny plant body.

Antlions

When I was growing up, I had a friend named Janey who shared with me a dislike for the seemingly interminable church services we were both forced to attend on sunny Sunday mornings in spring. One day we managed to sneak out of church early, and with nothing to do but hang around until the service was over, she asked if I would like to see something terrible. Of course I agreed, and she took me to the south side of the stone church and showed me a series of tiny pits, something like miniature volcanoes that had formed in the sandy soil by the side of the wall. "There," she said, "these are the death pits of antlions and they are truly GRUE-SOME INSECTS." She then sent me out to catch ants, and when I returned she dropped one into the pit. The poor ant struggled up the side, but the more desperately it climbed, the more the sandy sides of the pit slipped, forcing the ant ever down toward the base. And there, lurking just beneath the soil, was the dreadful antlion. To make matters worse, periodically the hideous unseen creature at the bottom of the pit would flick sand grains up toward the rim, making escape all but impossible. Finally, to Janey's eternal delight, a pair of tiny pinchers emerged from the sand and grabbed the poor ant and held it until it stopped moving. "Gruesome," she said. "Absolutely gruesome."

I too was fascinated, needless to say, and whenever we could the two of us would escape from the boring messages on the nature of sin salvation that took place within the church walls to witness the gory realities of the life-and-death struggles that took place no more than a few yards from the pulpit.

Janey might have been even more delighted had she known that the creature at the bottom of the pit was possessed of a pair of tubes running through its vicious pinchers with which the antlion injects a toxic, paralyzing fluid into the body of its prey, and that following paralysis, the creature sucks out the vital juices of the ant.

The monster in the sand pit is actually the larva of a far more benign insect that looks very much like the damselfly. The adult often appears at porch lights on summer nights and I'm afraid often falls victim to what is to my mind a far more ominous instrument of death—the pervasive suburban black light or bug light. These supposed insect controllers kill vast numbers of innocent creatures, including a number of rare and endangered night-flying moth species. Antlion adults, lacewings, moths, and many other delicate creatures of the night fall prey to the machine's indiscriminate electrical wires, whereas the intended victim, the mosquito, generally escapes unharmed.

One way to find antlion larvae is to search the dry soil under the eaves of your house. If you see a few pits about two inches across and you are inquisitive, you can scoop up the pit and search the soil for the larvae. Look for the large pinchers on the forehead. If you are feeling bloodthirsty, you might drop an ant into the pit à la Janey and watch the larva send its little sprays of sand.

Warbler Migration

No matter where you live, mid-spring ushers in one of the greatest and least-observed events of the natural world. For some six months the vast population of small, insect-eating birds known as warblers, which inhabit the northern half of the continent during summer, have been living in the subtropical and tropical forests of Central and South America. By February they begin to leave for the north, and from April to mid-May they will pass over the face of the United States on their way to the Canadian forests. Some of these species may stop and nest anywhere from Texas northward and may be observed from time to time during the summer, but spring is the best time to see them. Generally warblers will appear in any region just before the trees leaf out. Watch for them in mid-spring in the upper branches. They are highly active and are visible with the naked eye, but to appreciate their color and their bright individuality you will need binoculars. Warblers are so numerous, it is safe to say that at the proper period, every back yard with trees will at some point in the day have a loose flock of these brightly colored birds passing through. But be sure to look for them just before the leaves appear. Once the trees have fully leaved, they are difficult to see.

Black and White Warbler

Black and White Warblers

Watch for these birds on or around tree trunks. They are one of the easier species to identify. For one thing, since they feed on trunk-dwelling insects, they are often in full view; and for another, they are brilliantly striped in black and white, a little like a flying zebra. Their call is an unmistakable repetitious squeak that sounds very much like a wagon wheel in need of grease. Black and white warblers nest from south Texas north to Newfoundland. Food consists of a number of pest species, such as the gypsy moth and the brown-tailed moth. They have an interesting habit of circling tree trunks, vigorously checking into every possible nook and calling intensely all the while.

Yellow Warblers

The yellow warbler is the so-called wild canary of suburban back yards. It is a small bird, smaller than a canary, and is all yellow—no masks, caps, spots, or wing patches. The only other common yellow bird that you may see in your yard is the goldfinch, which has black on its wings and tail. Yellow warblers often nest near water, in willow thickets and the like; but if you have any good hedges on your grounds, any place that will provide a little protection, it is possible that this common bird will take up residence there.

Yellow-throat Warblers

The yellow-throat is another common yellow-colored warbler of suburban thickets. It looks like a yellow warbler except that the male has a definite black mask like a raccoon or a wood frog. If you are a bird novice, this may be one of the first warblers you will be able to recognize; the black mask is unmistakable, and these are also very active and almost tame warblers. If there is one near your house, and if you happen to wander near its nest, it will begin flitting around in the thickets calling with a sharp "chit" or "check."

Yellow-rumped Warblers

A loud "check" from bushes and trees at the side of your yard may also indicate the presence of yellow-rumped warblers. These are basically streaked, blue-gray birds with yellow spots on the cap and sides and a prominent yellow patch just above the tail. When they appear in your yard, they will likely appear in large numbers. Whether they will nest there is another matter; most individuals will continue to northern New England and on through the Canadian zone to the tree line. They will be back in the fall, however, and may remain in your region longer than most warblers, since they tend to feed on berries, especially bayberries. The common name for this bird used to be the myrtle warbler because of its fondness for myrtle or bayberry.

Palm Warblers

The palm warbler is more or less a city bird in the South. It can be seen mostly during the winter months, flitting around on the ground in parks and in yards in outlying urban areas. Like other warblers, it moves north in the spring to breed in the pine forests of Canada and northern New England. The bird spends most of its time on or near the ground and can be readily recognized by its tail-wagging habit. If you see a small bird with a chestnut-colored cap and a yellowish breast that wags its tail almost constantly, it's probably this species. On the other hand, if you see a bird in overgrown fields or in young pine or oak forests that wags its tail, it might be a prairie warbler. Watch for the bright yellow breast and the prominent black stripes in the prairie. The palm is a more subtle bird. If you live in an area where there are prairie warblers, you may hear them more often than you see them. The call is a trill or series of thin whistles that go up the chromatic scale monotonously.

Blue-winged Warblers

There is one other warbler that you may hear rather than see. The blue-winged generally share the same habitat as the prairie warbler—brushy edges and scrubby second-growth forests. Its call sounds more electrical than any of the other warbler calls to my ear. In an urban area it might be mistaken for some kind of obscure alarm buzzer. Basically, it is an inhaled and exhaled buzz that is nearly impossible to describe in words. Hear it once in the fields, however, and you will be able to remember it. The buzzer itself is a handsome, yellowish bird with blue-gray wings marked with two white wing bars. The breast is a clear yellow—no stripes, no dots.

Bird Song

What is true of the blue-wing is true of most of the warblers. The most obvious element of the influx of wood warblers in late May is not necessarily the appearance or the view that you will get of these bright birds but the sounds they make. There are years when because of freakish weather conditions they may not arrive until after the leaves have come out on the trees, in which case spotting them, even if you are adept at bird finding, is no easy task. But like most birds in spring, warblers are charged at this season with mating hormones and as a result are calling and singing furiously. You have but to identify the various songs to know that they have arrived. Although this may involve some work in the beginning, it is a satisfying experience to lie in bed at six o'clock on a May morning identifying the birds that have arrived in your maple trees during the night.

How the birds known as warblers got their English name is a mystery to me. Most of these tiny insect-eaters have a song that sounds more like an electrical buzzing than any other sound, and none of them, to my knowledge, actually warbles—that is an art that has been perfected by mockingbirds and the catbird. But the various buzzes of warblers come in definite rhythms and follow typical patterns, a few of which are rather musical. Some of the patterns can be learned by remembering the rhythm of certain English phrases. The yellow warbler, for example, says "sweet sweet, sweet, summer sweet." The chestnut-sided warbler has a similar phrase—"please, please, please ta meetcha," or in some renditions, "pleased to see you Miss Beecher." The ovenbird calls the word "teacher" emphatically three times, increasing the volume each time—"teacher, teacher, TEACHER," and the yellow-throat says "witchty-witchty-witchy-witch." This technique only works for a few of the species that will pass through your back yard during spring migration, but at least it accounts for some of the more common warblers you can expect.

There are species other than warblers for whom this method works. The towhee and the phoebe say their names quite clearly, and the brown thrasher, according to traditional birdlore, encourages the gardener and the farmer to hurry up with planting: "plough it, plough it, hoe it, hoe it, put it in, put it in" and so on. There are other versions, but the thrasher always says whatever it says in pairs. Flickers, according to some imaginative bird listeners, say "quick, quick, quick, quick," from the woods each April, and meadowlarks quite appropriately call out "spring of the year" again and again from nearby fields.

There is one other way to recognize bird songs if you happen to be musically inclined. When I first started learning warbler songs, I was at the same time interested in music, and I kept noticing similarities between the songs of certain birds and the phrasing of passages of music. I have forgotten most of the connections now, but I do remember that somehow the song of the black-throated green warbler used to remind me of the opening of a Sibelius symphony, which one I have forgotten. I also remember, and in fact still have the sense, that the eerie, almost mystical song of the veery was somehow associated in my mind with Johann Sebastian Bach. You don't have to be a student of music to make these connections; like any music, either classical or popular, bird songs does have a definite phrasing, and whatever association you make to remember the calls, no matter how farfetched, is certainly helpful.

Nests in Spring

Although it is easier to find the nests in early winter, nest finding in spring is more of a challenge and infinitely more rewarding, since the nests are in use. Even semiurbanized yards may have active nests of bluejays, robins, starlings, house sparrows, and mourning doves. Watch the behavior of the birds you see in your yard in order to find the nest. Any bird carrying material such as grasses or string or feathers in its beak is probably in the process of constructing a new nest, and if you track the path of the bird, you will probably find it. After that, you can observe the progression of activity there during the nesting season. Watch especially for courtship behavior, which, depending on the species, may involve elaborate gift exchanges (the gifts often consisting of nesting material), the construction of the nest itself, food begging, and, of course, singing. Once the birds have mated and the eggs are laid, activity will quiet down for a few weeks, and then after the young hatch, the hard work of providing sustenance begins. Watch for both males and females carrying food back to the nest.

If you are ambitious, or lucky, you can observe the raising of the young close at hand. For the ambitious, it is possible to set up an observation place in a nearby tree and spend an hour or so there each day observing (or photographing) the feeding activity. On the other hand, birds often make their nests in trees and shrubbery surrounding houses, and it is sometimes possible to get a good view of the action without leaving your bedroom.

For several years, for example, a wood thrush made a nest in a huge clump of rhododendrons just beyond the kitchen window of the house in which I grew up. I was able to watch the entire progress of bird behavior while eating breakfast, from early courtship to nest building, egg laying, hatching, rearing, and, finally, the first flights of the young. In another year a bluejay nested in a pine tree just below a bedroom window on the south side of the house, and in yet another year a starling raised a brood under a porch over the front door. More recently, a phoebe built a nest just under a trellis beside the back porch in my house. In spite of the endless passage of little children, the slamming of screen doors, and the presence of curious adults, the couple regularly raised two broods a year over a period of three or four years.

Interesting though nesting may be, suburban house-holders are often troubled by the presence of nesting birds. Nature centers where I have worked used to regularly receive complaints concerning woodpeckers battering houses in the early morning hours or calls about birds (usually robins) attacking cellar windows again and again. Needless to say, the birds have nothing against the house. The robins are invariably males, and since the house happens to be in *their* territory, they are merely fighting what they believe to be male intruders—in this case, their own reflections in cellar windows. The fighting can be halted by hanging curtains or taping newspapers over the windows for a few weeks during the breeding season. The woodpecker problem is a harder case. There is nothing much that can be done about it other than getting up each morning and squirting the offending bird with a garden hose or, in persistent cases covering the area with plastic.

One other little bit of nesting behavior you may notice later in spring is the figure of a large gray bird with white wings and tail patches chasing your cat across the lawn. Mockingbirds are generally considered to be birds of southern regions, but over the past few decades they have been extending their range and now nest as far north as New England. Mockers are excellent singers and highly territorial in their nesting behavior; you will see them singing and chasing each other throughout the spring mating season. Once the young have hatched, they become even more aggressive and will chase almost anything that comes into their territory, including that arch-enemy of songbirds, the house cat.

Mockingbird and Nest

Ornamental Trees and Shrubs

Unless you have built and landscaped your house yourself, it is likely that you will have inherited the plantings from the previous owner or owners. In some cases, this may mean that you have, in effect, inherited the original natural vegetation in the area—oaks, perhaps, or maples or sourgums. In other cases, this may mean that you have inherited nothing more than a sweep of highly fertilized, pesticided, and herbicided green lawn. There is, among the dwellers of suburbia, a species of individual who customarily evicts all native and non-native vegetation in order to maintain a quarter-acre of so of grass. Horror stories of some of the notorious evictions abound. I heard of one man who cut down ranks of fruiting berry bushes and twenty-five-year-old fruit trees simply because their presence made it difficult for him to turn his riding mower. In general, however, owners of suburban houses, even if they are not by nature gardeners, have planted a few trees and shrubs around the property. Following are a few common ones to watch for.

Dogwood

The various species of flowering dogwood seem to be among the more universally popular ornamental trees. Branches of the dogwood tree grow opposite each other in a regular pattern and look something like the antlers of a deer. The flowers, which appear in spring, have flat tops and are usually white, although there is a pink ornamental variety. Dogwood is a native tree in North America. When the tree in your yard goes into flower, watch the roadside woodlands around you for the wild ones; they are common in some sections of the country and make a splendid showing in the spring forests.

Horse Chestnut

If you live in an older suburb you may have in your yard or in some nearby yard a large tree that puts out white clusters of flowers in spring and spiky burs in the fall. The horse chestnut is more closely related to the Ohio buckeye than to the American chestnut tree—most of which were killed off in a blight in the early part of this century. The "chestnuts" are not edible and in fact are reported to be poisonous by some authorities. Nevertheless, they are a favorite with small children, who, given the opportunity, will collect hordes of them for chestnut fights or for more peaceful uses such as decorative necklaces.

Norway Maple

There are many species of maple native to the United States and Canada, but ironically, if you have a planted maple in your yard (as opposed to a wild one), it is likely to be a Norway maple, which is a native of Europe and western Asia. Horticulturalists have developed many different varieties of this species, but basically, the younger trees have red leaves and yellowish flower clusters in the spring. In the autumn the leaves will turn a pale yellow, whereas many native species turn a brilliant red. Like the dogwood, the leaves and branches are opposite.

Locust

Locust trees are reportedly gaining in popularity as ornamentals, although they are widely distributed in the wild as well. The black locust is tall and narrow, has irregularly placed branches, dark, reddish-brown bark, and pealike flowers. The closely related honey locust is also grown ornamentally, although in its wild state it boasts viscious three-forked spines on its branches and even on its trunk. This is not a tree that asks to be climbed or leaned against. Fortunately, a tamer, spineless variety has been developed by horticulturalists.

Kentucky Coffee Tree

The Kentucky coffee tree can be found in the wild from Canada south to Georgia and west to Kansas and Michigan, but it has been cultivated and planted in yards throughout the United States. It is closely related to the honey locusts, has the similarly divided leaves with many leaflets and white flowers, and curious bark with curlicue patterns or ridges and scales. Indians in the Midwest used to roast the beans from this tree and prepare a coffeelike beverage. White explorers along the Missouri picked up on the habit—thus the name.

Mountain Ash

The mountain ash is a native of Europe, but it was used in this country as an ornamental and has now escaped into the wild. It is still planted in yards and gardens, however. Brilliant red berries in the fall can be made into a tasty jelly. The fruit is also eaten by a number of birds and mammals, including grouse and white-tailed deer.

Arbor Vitae

Evergreen trees such as the arbor vitae, fir or spruce, and white pine periodically gain favor among nurserymen and home gardners only to lose favor again for a few decades. One of the perennial favorites is the arbor vitae, a cone-shaped tree with pale reddish bark that peels off in long strips and flat, fanshaped needles that look as if they have been recently ironed. If you have one of these on your property, you may have many; they were sometimes planted as full hedges during the 1920s and early 1930s. Arbor vitae are native to the American con-

Arbor Vitae

tinent, but there is an Asiatic species that is commonly used for ornamental plantings, so the arbor vitae you see in your yard and the one you see in an abandoned field may not be the same species.

Fir

Fir trees were popular ornamental trees in the New England region around the turn of the century. The ones that are still living are now grandiloquent old things with dark branches and shady underskirts. If you live in an older house and you have one on your property, you will know it immediately by its splendor; it will be the largest, most obvious natural element in your yard. Fir is also used as a Christmas tree, and some past resident who has taken advantage of the living Christmas tree idea may have planted a few younger ones around your property. The shiny green needles have white bands on their undersides, and the twigs are rounded and have a resin covering. Fir trees, along with various species of spruces, are responsible for the rich piny odor of the northern forests.

Spruce

Red spruce, white spruce, and an ornamental variety known as Alberta spruce may have been planted in your yard in recent years. The four-sided needles are short, about one inch long, and are distinctly needlelike. The introduced Norway spruce, which you may also have in your yard, has needles that are more flattened. Spruces are aromatic trees; the needles have the rich smell of northern forests and, not surprisingly, often attract northern finches during the winter season. If you don't already have some in your yard and you live in a northern area, you might try planting a few on the north side of your house. They make good windbreakers and will provide excellent shelter for bird feeders and bird-feeding areas.

SUMMER

THERE IS A CERTAIN RAKING LIGHT that you will see slanting over your lawn on early mornings toward the end of June. It is not the sharp light of late summer and early fall, nor is it the pale white light of winter. This is the rich, almost palpable light that is not only soft but infused, it seems, with life, as if the growing energies of the earth had expanded into the very air. Glance at the rays of light at an angle to the sun, and you will see that the air is filled with particles, little drifts of pollen, floating or dancing clusters of midges and mayflies, or the darting forms of dragonflies, robber-flies, bees, and other arthropods. The air is very often humid during this season, sometimes almost wet in its fullness, and there is nothing that grows that does not thrive in this moist, bright world. Although not every-thing is yet in flower, plants are at the zenith of expan-sion—their roots forcing their way ever deeper into the moist soil, their leaves spreading upward and outward.

Those first few bursts of energy of springtime seem isolated, hardy attempts at living in an unkind, cold world, compared to the rush of life that goes on in early June and July. All the living things of the temperate zone, as if conscious of the limitations of the growing season, are forcing themselves outward. And yet this veritable rush of life is no longer-lived than any other season. Even by mid-July, the bloom goes off the rose and the summer settles in. By August, the heat—so welcome in June and early summer—may become an annoyance, and by the middle of the month genuinely oppressive. But that does not diminish the beauty of June. In fact it may be that no matter how little contact you have with the natural world, the long light of June and early July may have its dominion—even over the most city-bound individuals. Studies have suggested that the interaction of long hours of summer light on the human pineal gland located in the forehead causes the release of hormones that create a sense of well-being at this time of year—most especially, it turns out, around the twenty-first of June, when the daylight is at its longest. Since we all seem to be victims (or benefactors) of this mystic chemistry, you might as well give in to it, go outdoors, and enjoy the little patch of planet that by late twentieth-century legal standards you are privileged to call "your" land.

Fireflies

One of the more pleasant memories of my childhood is of summer porches on the eastern shore of Maryland. Often in evening I would sit with my father on the wide verandah of my parents' summer place and watch the tiny flashing stars of fireflies rise from the hayfields surrounding the house. My father loved fireflies. He was steeped in Japanese culture and would often tell me Oriental fairy tales about these unique insects and describe the honor that Japanese culture ascribes to them. The first flash of light from the evening hayfield would always inspire him, as if it were something he had never before seen. Some nights we would simply sit in silence, rocking and watching the display.

The light that so moved my father has inspired scientific research as well. Unlike other forms of light, the luminescence given off by fireflies and related animals is cold light; there is no heat associated with it. The shine is caused by the secretion of an enzyme that is combusted by oxygen to form the light. The method is highly efficient. Electric lights are only about 10 percent energy-efficient, whereas firefly lighting approaches 100 percent and is, in comparison to firelight, gaslight, or electric light, entirely pollution free.

The light flashing is a mating ceremony. If you watch a single firefly cross your lawn, you may be able to see that it flashes a certain number of times—depending on the species involved. What you will not notice unless you search it out is that somewhere down in the grass there is another firefly, a female, flashing a signal of her own to attract the male. As is often the case in the dog-eat-dog world of nature, this seemingly innocuous system of communication has been put to other uses. There is one species of predatory firefly that waits in the grass, signaling like a female, but when the unsuspecting, sex-starved male descends to mate, it is consumed by the predatory trickster.

One of the requirements of a good firefly field is long grass. If you have a perfectly trimmed lawn, perfectly trimmed hedges and flower and vegetable gardens, you may not have so many fireflies unless there is open land next door or nearby. I have a meadow on the north side of my house that I purposely leave uncut through June in order to encourage firefly populations. It is perhaps simply a replay of an old script, but I like very much to sit on the back porch on late spring and early summer evenings and watch the lightning bugs rise over the meadow and tell my little children stories about fireflies.

Mosquitoes

There is an axiom abroad that says something about the lack of free lunch in an ecological system. Nowhere is this perhaps more clear than in June, when the mosquito season is upon you. If you do not mow your lawn or clip your hedges, you will in all likelihood be able to experience the beauty of the fireflies. But if you walk through the long grass on those same limpid, warm nights, or if you dare to sit out on your patio, you are also likely to experience the bites of mosquitoes. A clear lawn, harshly trimmed hedges, and few trees might free you from inordinate numbers of these pests, but if you take this control method to its extreme, you might as well pave over the yard or give up altogether and move to the city.

Mosquitoes are the one pest among the many potential pests described in this book—skunks, raccoons, squirrels, mice, and the like—that are difficult to defend. They make an otherwise pleasant evening outdoors all but impossible in some sections of the country during the seasons in which they are active. In northern regions, black flies by day and mosquitoes by night have managed to keep whole nations of vacationers, and local people imprisoned behind walls or screens.

And yet, like the flowers and the butterflies, they too have their seasons. Black fly season in northern areas can sometimes be measured in a matter of weeks, and although some species of mosquitoes may be around all summer, generally they hatch out in June and are gone by August. If you can learn to live with the inconvenience for a month or so, if you do not accept the mosquito hordes of a June night as the norm, then you can enjoy your yard more at night throughout the rest of the year.

Depending on where you live, you may experience several blossomings of different species of mosquitoes. Woodlands have their species, open fields or wet areas have theirs, so unless you live in a desert region, at one point during the summer you are bound to be bothered by them. When a mosquito lands on you, if you allow it to live long enough, you can begin to see the differences in the species without much study. Generally the striped mosquitoes are woodland dwellers, whereas those with plain brown bodies live in marshes or fields. The mosquitoes that bite you are the females, and the reason they bite you is to get the protein in your blood, which they need for egg laying. If it's any consolation, mosquitoes also bite birds and other mammals; in fact, many species will feed on human beings only reluctantly, and some not at all, even if there's no other blood source around. Once the female mosquito has engorged herself on your blood, she will return to a sheltered spot to sleep off her meal, a little like a stuffed lioness. The eggs that she lays and the larvae that emerge from the eggs have to have water to survive, even though the larvae are not truly aquatic insects. The wrigglers you see on the surface of ponds and puddles are all air breathers. One way to protect yourself from these pests is to make certain that there is no standing water around in your yard for them to lay their eggs in. This cleanup program may be rendered useless if you live near water, but if you don't, it is worth a try.

Another technique is to learn more about the cycles of the species of mosquitoes that you have in your yard.

SUMMER

Different species of mosquitoes have different biting cycles, or flying cycles. Some fly in the early morning hours, whereas some hunt only in evening or very late at night. If you can spot which species is active during a certain period and then avoid being outside during those hours, you will not have much trouble. You don't have to identify the insects by name to do this; you just have to be able to recognize a few of the field marks—size, for example, and color or pattern. As I have pointed out elsewhere, one control method that does *not* work is the black light or bug light. Despite commercial claims, these kill thousands of harmless and in some cases rare and endangered species of insects and only knock out a few individual mosquitoes. Another useless control, except perhaps during health emergencies, are town spraying programs. Spray trucks, moving along town roads misting the trees, kill very few of the billions of mosquitoes that are lurking in the dank swamps, woods, and fields beyond the reach of the sprayers. Aerial spraying programs, although arguably somewhat more efficient, may strike one species for a while, but another may hatch no more than a few days after the planes and helicopters have passed over. Furthermore, as any local beekeeper will tell you, the sprays kill hundreds of innocent species of insects. Some of the chemicals used are at least suspected as a human health hazard, and many, though still legal, are downright dangerous.

Amphibians in the Grass

I have noticed that there is another advantage to having long grass in the meadow on the north side of my property. Apart from the fact that there are a number of beautiful field wildflowers growing there, and apart from

Pickerel Frog

the fact that I can see dragonflies, fireflies, and butterflies throughout the month of June, and hear the great rolling chorus of bush katydids and grasshoppers in late summer, I find that the very act of managing this little piece of grassland is in itself an exploration.

Over the past few years I have become an addict of scything. It is not only a good exercise and a better, more ecological way, in my view, of mowing grass, it also affords you a closer look at the things that live in longer grass. Of these humble creatures, my favorites are the frogs and toads that I unhouse while I am scything. You don't have to be a scyther to find these amphibians, but the act of walking over each square yard of your land, cutting down grass as you go, tends to send them hopping. Errant individuals are forever bounding ahead of the blade with spectacular leaps. They are to me like small bright jewels amidst the green of the vegetation.

SUMMER

Periodically I catch them, just to admire the patterning on their backs, the fine turn of their legs, and the bright spectacular eyes.

In the area where I live the most common grass-dwelling frog is the pickerel frog. The "spots" on the back of this frog are shaped like squares, and if you catch one and turn it over you will see bright yellow or orange on the inside of the hind legs. It is possible to find these frogs in your yard even if you live far from water. After they leave their breeding areas in marshes and permanent ponds, they tend to wander in upland meadows in search of food. In fall they will return to the marshes and ponds to hibernate for the winter.

The similarly marked leopard frog also wanders far from water after breeding and may also turn up in the longer grass of your back yard. Leopard frogs have round spots as opposed to squared ones and are white under the legs. This is a very successful frog as far as distribution goes; it can be found throughout the United States, except for California and the northwest, and it is believed to be the most widely distributed amphibian in the United States. Both of these frogs eat small insects and other invertebrates and are in turn eaten by some of the other meadow-dwelling denizens, such as foxes, hawks, skunks, and snakes. The pickerel frog, however, like the toad, secretes an acrid fluid from its skin that may irritate the membranes in the mouth of some predators. The leopard frog, by contrast, may be consumed by human beings. These frogs do not have as much meat on them as the more commonly eaten legs of the bull-frog, but they are passable. My friend Hatch Griggs, the wild-food enthusiast, in saner moments used to work as a biology teacher at a private school near where we lived in Connecticut. Periodically in odd seasons he would invite me over for frog's legs broiled with wild thyme, which as far as I am concerned was something of a memorable dish. I found out later that the frogs were from his school laboratories. Leopard frogs are commonly sold by biological supply houses. If you haven't seen one in your back yard, you probably saw one in your high-school biology classes.

If you live in an area where there are woods or a good supply of ornamental shade trees, you may also find in the long grass a beautiful green jewel of a frog with rounded pads on its feet. This is the young of the far more interestingly patterned gray tree frog. You may also find the adult lying along the branch of one of your trees, although the camouflage of these frogs is so variable and so perfect they are not easy to see unless you can track them down by their calling. The color of gray tree frogs may range from the gray of their name to green or very pale gray. They are squat frogs, larger than spring peepers, about two inches in length, with multi-patterned beautiful eyes (if you can ever get close enough to see them). On sultry days in June, often before a rain shower, it seems, you can hear the rich, melodious call of these frogs. The sound is very birdlike; one would expect warblers to sing in this manner—if they warbled. The call is a short, ascending trill that sounds to me very like a well-aged open-hole flute. There is no sound quite like it, and coming as it does, on the warm air of a June afternoon, it carries with it an overtone of fertility and ripeness. The callers are also somewhat ventriloquistic, it seems to me. I once spent the better part of a June evening trying to find a singing gray tree frog that turned out to be no more than a few feet away.

If you have a pond nearby, the song may be quite another matter. I used to live near a mill pond in Old Lyme, Connecticut, and nightlong throughout the summer the gray tree frogs kept up their chorus. The noise on still nights might have seemed oppressively prolonged were it not for the fact that I am thoroughly partial to frog song.

Other Frogs

From time to time while I am out scything I also come across less commonly seen upland frogs. During wet seasons, even though I live half a mile from the nearest pond, I have occasionally spotted bullfrogs and green frogs in the meadow. The bullfrogs are generally the largest frogs you will find in your yard, about six inches or so when they are full grown. They are an overall green color and have smooth backs. The green frog, which also appears in the meadow from time to time, has two ridges running down its back and is smaller, although the adult greens and young bulls may be about the same size. If you live near a pond, the bullfrog will make its presence known by its night chorus. In one place I used to hear them rumbling in the distance like some kind of obscure, deep-throated generator. The racket created by the bulls at a pond near my parent's summer house on the Eastern Shore of Maryland was nearly deafening and, true to frog form, went on all night. Late one night a crazy brother of mine went down to the pond and shouted at them to shut up. They did. But as soon as he got back to the house, they started up again. The next night he went down with his .22 and started firing blindly at the water. The frogs shut up for a while, but on return he had his gun taken away and was grounded for a week by my parents. The indifferent frogs continued to call throughout the summer.

If you live south of the Mason Dixon line and have a house near a pond or a swamp, this problem of frog calling can become fairly intense. A good healthy swamp on a hot night in the South can become a cacophony of barks, rasps, groans, snorts, snorings, and rattles as leopard frogs, pickerel frogs, tree frogs, chorus frogs, toads, and cricket frogs run through their routines with unceasing froggy dementia. It is a madness worth making a trip to hear, although I am not sure I would want to live near such a place—much as I love frog calls.

Air Patrol

Given the ineffectiveness of most manmade pest controls, it is perhaps comforting to know that there is a dedicated group of birds that makes its living by consuming flying insects, including mosquitoes. Swifts, martins, and swallows by day, and nighthawks and whippoorwills by night are forever patroling the summer skies in search of food, even in suburban areas. You have but to lie on your back in your yard on a summer afternoon and watch the sky to see them work. Except in the most heavily urbanized areas, you will see at least a few swallows or swifts pass by, and by night even in cities you may be able to see nighthawks and swifts. Some of these acrobatic flyers, such as the barn swallow, the martin, and the cliff swallow, need specialized nesting areas. But others have adapted well to city life. Nighthawks, for example, regularly nest on the flat roofs of buildings in small cities throughout the United States, and at dusk on summer evenings I have seen hordes of chimney swifts descending into the chimney of an insurance company in the town near where I live.

Some of these flyers are difficult to recognize, since they are perpetually on the wing. But there are a few common ones that, with only a few field marks, you can spot even at great distance.

SUMMER

Swallows

If you have open land and have set out bluebird nest boxes or tree swallow nest boxes, and if there are tree swallows anywhere near you, chances are they will set up house. They adapt well to suburban environments and are easily recognized by their cream white bellies and chests and greenish-black backs. They are especially common in areas where there is a certain amount of water.

Another relatively common swallow of suburban areas is the barn swallow. Generally these are birds of open country and farms; in fact, they are almost a regular feature of any working farm, since the barns and outbuildings provide nesting space, and the cows and other livestock often attract the flies that these swift-flying birds feed upon. Barn swallows are the easiest swallows to recognize in flight; they have the classic forked tail of the swallow, and since the tail is an active aerial control mechanism, it is readily observable. If your house has been located in former farm country and if there are even a few farms left in your area, you are bound to see barn swallows. There used to be hordes of them over the meadow on the north side of my house. They nested in an abandoned barn across the road. One winter a March storm caved in the barn, but, not to be defeated, the swallows returned that year and nested in the ruins. Unfortunately, the fast-suburbanizing town in which I live deemed the barn an attractive nuisance, and wrecking crews appeared one morning and carted it off to the dump. I haven't seen barn swallows over my meadow since. *Sic transit gloria mundi*.

Purple Martins

According to bird folklore, the undisputed lord of all the mosquito consumers is the purple martin. This is the largest of the swallows you will see over your yard, some seven or eight inches long. They are generally dark in color, black with a tinge of blue in sunlight. Martins, like tree swallows, are avid box nesters and in fact will dwell in large apartmentlike houses constructed especially with martins in mind. So great is the reputation of these birds as mosquito eaters that ads for the houses in bird magazines often feature the martin houses as a serious method of pest control. Martins do consume huge numbers of mosquitoes in areas such as salt marshes where there are high numbers of these insects, but they also rely on other flying things as a food source, many of which are thoroughly harmless. Not only that, the martin housing projects, like some of their human counterparts, are not always success stories. Species that bird lovers consider less desirable, such as starlings and house sparrows, will also nest communally, or at least take up enough space in the martin apartments to drive off the insect-consuming swallows.

Chimney Swifts

While you are watching the sky over your yard for swallows, if you see a cigar with wings pass by, you have seen a chimney swift. The appearance of this bird in flight—the bow and arrow shape, or the flying cigar—is pretty much unmistakable. They are fast birds, seemingly forever twittering to themselves as they pass to and fro over their feeding areas, and they are very common, as I have said, in suburban and even urban areas. They nest inside chimneys, fastening the nest to the rough walls with mud and saliva, and in some rural areas, where the fireplaces of summer houses are used only occasionally, they can cause smoke backups. During migrations, in spring and late summer, they form huge, swirling flocks. It is one of the small spectacles of the suburban wildlife world, I think, to watch one of these great flocks curl into a chimney at dusk to their communal roost. They circle chattering madly for a long time before descending to the inner depths. Once they begin to enter, they will form a huge circulating gyre or funnel of birds, until finally, sometime after dark, the last twittering individual enters, and the sky above the chimney goes silent.

Flycatchers

Although they are not half so acrobatic as the swifts and the swallows, flycatchers also do their bit for pest control in the back yard. The most diligent of these, or at least the most common in suburban areas, is the phoebe (pp. 24–26), but depending on where you live, you may also spot great crested flycatchers, kingbirds, and, in less developed suburbs, other woodland-dwelling flycatchers, such as the wood peewee. Whereas swallows and swifts continually course through the air in search of food, flycatchers wait on an exposed branch or post and watch for their prey. When an apparent meal flies past, they will leave the perch, swoop down on the insect, and return to the branch to eat and watch for more. Occasionally you will see them miss on the first shot and chase down the insect with a fluttering, darting attack, but generally they are successful on the first swoop.

The phoebe is the easiest of these birds to recognize, because of its tail-wagging habit, but the kingbird also regularly visits back yards within its range. It exhibits all the characteristic flycatcher hunting techniques, but it is also fairly aggressive within its territory and seems to have an inherent dislike for larger birds. You can often see kingbirds chasing hawks and crows. If you have any old farmers or country people left in your neighborhood, they will probably tell you that the kingbird eats more than its share of bees. The grandfather of a friend of mine used to shoot kingbirds, or beehawks as he called them, because he believed they were destroying his hives. They do in fact eat a few bees, but they also include many other flying insects in their diet.

One of the common sounds that you may hear in your yard in late spring and early summer is a sort of drawn-out screech—the call of the great crested flycatcher. This is a rather plainly marked bird with a yellowish breast and a brownish back. What you usually see, if you see one, is a flash of yellow mixed with the reddish brown on the wings and tail. The easiest identification of this flycatcher is its screech. Once you learn to recognize the call, you will hear it all the time if you have crested flycatchers on your land. A little bit of acquired knowledge such as this, something that happens all the time in the study of nature, brings up an interesting question. One wonders, after learning to hear crested flycatchers or phoebes, how you could have been deaf to so common a sound for so many years.

Another common call of late spring and early summer is the beautifully haunting song of the wood peewee. This is another one of those species with a near-perfect common name. The bird lives in wooded areas, and it quite clearly enunciates its name, in a drawn-out but unmistakable fashion. Although this is definitely a bird of woodlands, it may be present in older suburbs where the trees are larger and the grounds of the houses are wooded.

Nightflyers

Once the swifts, swallows, and flycatchers are in their nests or roosting spots for the night, the whippoorwills and nighthawks emerge to take up the work of insect

SUMMER

Nighthawk

control. Generally both species eat larger insects than do their daytime counterparts; but, since mosquitoes are an all-too-common insect of the night, they figure heavily in the diet of the whippoorwill and may also be eaten by the higher-flying nighthawks.

The whippoorwill is another one of those birds that you will hear more often than you will see, and the likelihood of your hearing it appears to be diminishing rapidly. It is essentially a bird of the forest, pine forests especially, and unless you have a good woodlot nearby, you are not likely to hear the bird. On the other hand, on more than one summer evening, during the migration period of whippoorwills I used to hear them calling from a brushy area on an estate no more than a mile

Nighthawk

from the George Washington Bridge in New York City. I was also nearly knocked down by one in the same general area one night. Like a giant bat, it flitted out from some trees, brushed past my face so close at hand that I could feel the wind from its wings, and then flapped off into the gloom soundlessly. It was fortunate, I believe, that I knew about whippoorwills at the time, or I might have believed that the messenger of death had come to fetch me. It was a slightly disconcerting experience.

By contrast, you may both see and hear nighthawks over your yard even if you live in a relatively urbanized region. They look a little like gigantic, high-flying swallows and have the same beautiful twisting flight. They also call frequently while they are aloft—listen for a sharp "peent" not unlike the "peent" of the woodcock. Nighthawks, like swallows, often fly in small groups, so if you spot one of these slim-winged birds overhead, watch the sky for more. By late summer, nighthawks begin to migrate south; toward late afternoon in late August, watch the sky and you may see them passing.

The flight of these birds is also very like the flight of bats and because of this was once responsible for one of those minor shocks of observation that nature watchers sometimes experience. I was observing the flight of bats on one evening through a pair of binoculars when the clear image of a monster bat flew into the image area of the glass. I was more or less in a half-reverie at the time, simply enjoying the aesthetics of the bat turns, and the vision of this otherworldly creature—so huge and so out of place—threw me into a confusion of time and place. I thought for a second I had been transported to the Indian subcontinent and was witnessing the flight of the giant fruit-eating foxbats. It took me a second or two to realize it was simply a nighthawk.

SUMMER

Dragonflies

I remember looking out over the meadow in front of one house where I lived and seeing a veritable air force of dragonflies. Never before had I seen so many in one place. They darted from left to right across the meadow, hovered in mid-air, streamed right to left, north to south, rose vertically (or so it seemed) and alighted briefly on the longer stems of grasses, only to take off again to hunt the airways. I realize now that these were probably a single species, the green darner, which is migratory and can gather in considerable numbers in late summer and early autumn. But it is possible to see a wide variety of dragonflies in lesser congregations over the gardens of your back yard.

There are 5,000 to 10,000 species of dragonflies in the world, so I will leave it to you and your insect guide books to sort out which species you have above your yard. But without naming names, it is possible to learn the differences between a few of the common ones that you will probably see during the course of a summer. One of the most obvious is the large green darner described above. It is by far one of the larger dragonflies and is colored a bright green and has clear two-inch-long wings. Watch for them especially in late summer.

There is also a common species, found in areas near water, that has clear wings marked with dark patches at the tip, center, and near the body. Another common species has a handsome dark red or maroon body. Other field marks or differences to watch for are the clear wings, gray bodies, and of course different sizes. It may seem impossible to sort out the differences in these fast-flying insects, but once you learn the common characteristics of the ones that are in your yard, it's just a question of finding out the name in an insect identification book, preferably one with color plates.

Green Darner Dragonfly

If you live anywhere near water, there is another insect you may see in your yard that looks very much like a dragonfly. The damselfly has all the dragonfly characteristics—elongated body, clear double wings, and speedy flying pattern; however, when the damselfly lands, it holds its wings aloft over its body. Dragonflies hold their wings out flat or horizontally when they are at rest.

There used to be a lot of nasty rumors concerning dragonflies and damselflies. The worst of these suggested that these insects patrol the world in search of bad little boys and girls, sewing up the eyes and ears of incorrigible liars and miscreants. Another legend suggests that these insects tend to the health and well-being

SUMMER

of snakes by either doctoring them or, alternatively, feeding them. Snake doctor, snake feeder, and devil's darning needle are common folk names for these insects, all reflecting these beliefs.

Dragonflies, in fact, hardly fit the legends. They are efficient predators that catch any number of insects on the wing, including mosquitoes. If you watch carefully, you can sometimes see them make a kill. They use their legs as a net or grabber, scoop up the prey while still in flight, and transfer it to their mouths. In spite of their ominous stingerlike tails, they do not sting. They can bite, however, and the larger ones may nip if you catch them. On the other hand, catching one of these speedy devils in your bare hands is no easy task, so there isn't much to worry about.

Summer Weeds

If you have a garden, or even if you raise a few annuals or perennials along the foundation of your house, you are bound to have a few unwanted guests among your plants. Some of these have wings, some, such as voles and chipmunks, burrow relentlessly toward your favorite bulbs or perennials, and some have leaves and a seemingly eternal vitality. Try to be tolerant; except for the fact that they grow where you don't want them to, weeds are interesting and, in their own way, beautiful plants. Following are a few common garden invaders.

Purslane

Like many of the plants we refer to as weeds, purslane was introduced into the New World; unlike most of the plants that came over with the first Europeans, however, it was brought here intentionally. Purslane is considered a delicacy in many sections of Europe and Asia;

it is sold as a green in markets and has been a staple in some places for at least 2,000 years.

It is an easy weed to recognize. It has a fat, succulent stem and thick leaves that grow in a rounded starlike pattern. Left on its own, it will spread out with a disorganized, rambling growth. Given a chance, it will take over your garden; so pull it up when it is half-grown and eat it raw with salad, or, if you have enough, cook it as you would spinach. Better yet, let it go if you dare. I have a friend who experiments with alternative food crops in his garden. One year he found himself short on weeding time and quite by accident grew only purslane. Needless to say, with absolutely no work he had tremendous yields. The next year he grew rows of it and now cultivates dandelion, sorrel, mustard, lamb's quarter, and other noxious weeds, all of them edible.

Mustard

One of the other weeds that will undoubtedly come up in your neglected garden or weed patch at some point is the mustard, which, like so many of our so-called weeds, is another one of those useful escapees in the New World. Black mustard, one of any number of mustard species to appear in your yard, produces bright yellow flowers in the spring; look for the four petals in the shape of a cross, and later in the season, look for the inch-long four-sided pods. Inside the pods you will find small dark brown seeds that, if bitten into, will give off the sharp, pungent taste of mustard. Black mustard is commonly cultivated in Europe and Asia as a salad plant; early in the spring the leaves make an excellent addition to a traditional salad of boring, store-bought Boston lettuce. You can even make a wild mustard condiment from the seeds; simply grind them up, add a little water, and mix in flour to the right consistency.

SUMMER

There is another use for mustard seeds. If you happen to have a canary or a parakeet, you can collect the seeds or, after the stems dry, the whole stalk, pods and all, and hang the stalks in the cage. Your birds will appreciate the treat. You can also gather a bunch of mustard stalks late in the summer, dry them, and hang them up near your bird feeder in winter.

Pokeweed

Although you probably won't find it in your garden, another inhabitant of the weed patch is a tall, coarse herb with large alternating leaves, purple stems, and clusters of dark purple berries. Pokeweed is the subject of considerable debate among wild-plant connoisseurs. Some authorities state that the berries and roots are deadly poisonous and the plant should be avoided as a food source. Others consume the young leaves and even the meat of the berry without complaint. The large root and the seeds inside the berries are toxic, but no one seems to agree exactly how toxic. In any case, it is generally believed that the young greens are edible, and in fact in some European countries the plant is cultivated. Poke salad was once fairly standard fare in some sections of the South and is the subject of at least one formerly popular Cajun melody—"Poke Salad Annie." The purple berries have an abundance of purple juice and make excellent face paint for children's Indian encampments. One year at a birthday party I set up my children with a makeshift Indian village. To prepare the tribe for celebration, I showed the children one pokeweed and told them to scour the property for more. Within minutes they had found more pokeweed than I could ever have located on my own and most of them had smeared their faces a lurid purple.

The plant is not hard to identify. It is fairly large—

Pokeweed

along with American bamboo, it is one of the larger herbaceous plants in any region. The soft green leaves may be as much as ten inches long and are shaped something like a large African spearhead. It is the clusters of purple berries that are characteristic, however. Once you learn to spot them you will see pokeweed in almost every weed patch.

Goosefoot

There are approximately sixty species of goosefoot growing in the United States, most of them found in the Midwest from Canada south to Kentucky, Virginia, and Delaware. The plant looks a lot like lamb's quarters, belongs to the same family, and in fact grows in pretty much the same general areas—disturbed soils such as your garden or flower beds. Members of this family are wonderful seed bearers; a single large plant may contain as many as 75,000 individual seeds. And, not surprisingly, the goosefoot is a source of food for a number of local songbirds, including doves, juncos, lark longspurs, sparrows, and goldfinches. The seeds are also consumed by mammals such as chipmunks and other ground squirrels.

Although many of the common "weeds" that you may find were introduced, goosefoot is a native American plant and may have been used by the Indians as a food plant. There was once an interesting archeological dig not far from where I lived; along with the bones of game animals and the remains of nuts and berries, the most common plant uncovered in the dig were seeds from plants in the goosefoot family. The site was used by the local Indians over 8,000 years ago, so it is clear that goosefoot has a long history as a food plant. In all likelihood, the seeds were added to the elaborate Indian stews that often contained everything from blueberries to venison.

Yarrow

Early in the spring, sometimes even before the grass turns green, if you have a somewhat weedy lawn you may find a small bunch of feathery leaves in your backyard.

Yarrow

SUMMER

Crush them and they will give off a sharp pinelike odor. Later in the summer, when this plant flowers, you will see the bright white flower clusters that identify this aromatic plant as yarrow. The individual flowers have five petals, but they crowd together at the top of the plant in a broad flat-topped cluster. In some individuals, the flower cluster is pink instead of white.

You can make a tea from the leaves of yarrow; simply place a few pinches of crushed dried or fresh leaves in a teapot, fill it with boiling water, and let the concoction steep for five minutes or more. The tea is not without its dangers, however. Although people I know who have had yarrow tea have experienced no ill effects, this beverage was commonly used during the Middle Ages to conjure up visions of the devil. I know one individual, a young, wild-haired man, who would eat or drink almost anything in quest of visions, who used to drink yarrow tea specifically for that purpose. I remember him complaining that in spite of the quantities of tea that he drank, he never did see anything out of the ordinary.

Yarrow was brought into this country in all likelihood specifically because of its many supposed medicinal uses. One of these uses accounts for the plant's botanical name, *Achillea*. Supposedly a decoction of the leaves would serve to heal wounds received in battle. According to legend, the man who discovered this property of yarrow was none other than Achilles, though little good it did him when he took an arrow in his heel at the battle of Troy.

Orange Hawkweed

Between your house and the sidewalk or the street, between your house and your neighbor's, or a neighboring woodlot, or field, or empty house lot, in overgrown lawns, in little unmowed patches under fences, anywhere, in fact, that the dandelion or similar "weeds" grow, you are likely to find hawkweed. It is one of those ubiquitous American plants able to work its way into even the most unlikely places. I found some growing in downtown Boston one year, not far from the bus stations and the Common. I also saw it once in the gutter of an old house in which I stayed for a while near Amherst, Massachusetts, growing in the accumulation of leaves and other organic matter that had collected at one end of a decidedly askew gutter. And if the orange hawkweed doesn't make it to your yard, it is likely that one of its cousin hawkweeds will—the Canada hawkweed, the mouse-eared, the rough, or the panicled hawkweed. These other hawkweeds have yellow flowers in place of the orange, but in all species the flower heads are dandelionlike, or daisylike.

All told, there are some fifty species of this interesting weed found in the United States. Although the leaves and seeds are eaten by a number of species of upland game birds such as grouse and a few mammals such as deer and rabbits, to my mind the interesting thing about this plant, especially the devil's paintbrush, is its beauty. Unfortunately, unless you have a wide expanse of lawn that you are willing to leave unmowed, you may never be able to experience the plant in its splendor. While it does have a certain mundane appeal as an individual, when a group of these hawkweeds get together, and especially when they cover an entire mountain meadow or upland pasture, they can turn a full acre or more a flaming orange from June through September. I used to allow a small patch of them to flower in a corner of my yard along with the robin's plantain and dandelion and then cut them down after they had gone to seed. While not the perfect greensward of most suburban homes (it was never that in any case), the lawn seemed none the worse because of their presence. Try leaving a few in your yard; it will make you appreciate the great swathes of color that appear along highways and in abandoned fields.

Back-yard Mammals

Winter is the best time of year to follow the comings and goings of the mammals that visit your back yard. Tracks in the snow often reveal more than you can ever determine from firsthand observation, since many species of mammals are nocturnal and only emerge to feed and go about their business after you have gone to sleep. Nevertheless, during the summer mammals that hibernate or go into a prolonged torpor in winter become active, and because many of these same winter-dormant animals happen to be diurnal, there is a good possibility that you will get a chance to see a few during the summer months. That may seem an unfortunate circumstance to some landholders. A few of these dirunal mammals that you find in the back yard, such as woodchucks and chipmunks, are considered pests. But even if your local mammals are pesky, try to be tolerant; after all, you are living in *their* territory, not vice versa.

Woodchucks

Early one summer evening I was sitting at the dining-room table looking over the yard and gardens when I noticed a fat brown mammal waddling toward the vegetable garden. With a sinking heart, I watched as it moved toward my carefully tended lettuce and beans; I knew that I would be facing a protracted war with a woodchuck that season. Fortunately, even as I watched, a brown streak left the porch, blurred across the yard, and set to scrambling through the beans and the squashes. The dog, a vigilant terrier with a deep-seated aversion to woodchucks, had spotted the villain at the same time. He missed catching that particular individual but so terrorized it that it never returned, nor have any of its relatives. If you have a garden, and you also have a woodchuck, it might be advisable to also get a terrier; a single woodchuck can wipe out an entire season's productivity.

In spite of their predilection for beans and lettuce, I am rather fond of woodchucks. I like their determined, slow, yet alert style, their rich coloration, their bright eyes, and their ability to survive even in what appears to be the most fully developed suburban areas. Given a choice, the woodchuck or groundhog prefers rural regions, open meadows, hayfields; but in those many agricultural areas that have been turned into suburbs, it continues to endure and can often be seen feeding along the edges of major highways leading to urban areas. The Taconic Parkway and the Merritt Parkway outside of New York City are famous examples.

Woodchucks hardly need description. They are about twenty-four inches long, usually fat, and have rounded ears and short legs. They live in underground dens that contain a network of tunnels, runways, and rooms, some of which are used for sleeping, some as toilets, and some as hibernating or birthing chambers. All told, a well-used woodchuck den may involve forty or fifty feet of underground space. Unless you have a lot of land, you probably won't have a den on your property, but if there is open land anywhere near you and there are woodchucks in your area, they will undoubtedly dig a den or two there, especially if there are a lot of gardens in your neighborhood. Woodchucks are particularly fond of tender green vegetation. They will consume vast amounts of weeds in the wild and will also eat insects, but given the opportunity, they prefer beans. Although they live underground, they are excellent tree climbers. My terrier has treed any number in his time.

Chipmunks

Another burrower you may find somewhat closer to home is the chipmunk. These small ground squirrels can be found in almost any area that has a reasonable amount of cover. Watch for them along stone walls, in the corners of your gardens, under or around fences, and in fact almost anywhere except open fields or wet areas. They live in tunnels that, like the burrows of the woodchuck, may have several chambers for different uses. The entrance to the tunnel, unlike the piled, raw earth of the opening of the woodchuck den, is a neat little hole about two inches across, the type of hole children always refer to as a snake hole. (Snakes don't live in holes, however.) Chipmunks carry away the diggings from their tunnels, so you won't see any excavated material near the entrance. There may be several exit or back doors to the chipmunk tunnel.

Food consists primarily of nuts, seeds, bulbs, berries, and other plant material, but chipmunks will also eat slugs and insects, and given the opportunity, they will consume the eggs of birds and reportedly will kill other small mammals. During the winter chipmunks retire to their underground nests, but unlike the woodchuck, which is a true hibernator, they do not go into the deep torpor of hibernating animals. They sleep a lot, but they will wake periodically to eat from the stored food chambers, and when the weather is warm enough, they will emerge to feed. Watch for them under your bird feeder on warm winter days.

Chipmunks are perky little animals that seem to be highly skittish, but can be tamed easily. There was an old woman in my hometown known as the Chipmunk Queen. Through her feeding programs and by bringing in live-trapped chipmunks, she had encouraged a virtual city of these animals. They would regularly feed from her hand, and some would run up her legs to take seeds that she held in her mouth (her kisses, she used to call them) or feed from seeds spread on her shoulder, lap or open hand. If you were careful, her chipmunks would even take food from the outstretched palms of wild young boys, an act of great faith on their part, in my opinion. If you so desire, you may be able to tame a few of your local chipmunks in the same manner, although any more than a few chipmunks can cause considerable problems in your garden. They do enjoy bulbs and can wreak havoc with lawns and flower beds by their incessant tunneling.

Thirteen-lined Ground Squirrels

A species closely related to the chipmunk is found in the western states, but in the plains region the common rodent of lawns and developed areas may be the thirteen-lined ground squirrel, an animal whose range appears to be expanding. Watch for them in open areas throughout the prairie region. Thirteen-lined ground squirrel species may feed on birds eggs as well as corn and wheat. But they also eat large numbers of grasshoppers and other destructive insects. They share the range and habitat with another ground-dwelling rodent, the pocket gopher, which has a poor reputation as a crop destroyer. Pocket gophers are stout and short-necked and have a reddish coloration, whereas the thirteen-lined ground squirrel has conspicuous stripes and spots running down its back.

Back-yard Bats

What the rat is to city dwellers, its insect-eating rural counterpart, the bat, is to suburban and rural people. The poor reputation in both cases, but most especially in the case of the bat, is, in my opinion, unjustified. The rat, the more destructive and pestilential of the two, is or can be a real problem when its number swells. But as long as you keep your distance, bats are for the most part harmless. They *are* among those local suburban mammals that carry rabies, but dogs, cats, skunks, raccoons, and foxes pose a far greater hazard, and unlike these other mammals, bats studiously avoid human contact. They do *not* become tangled in your hair, they do *not* suck blood, and their jaws are so weak they can barely break the skin if by chance they attempt to bite you. Since they are not attack animals, in order to be bitten, you have to catch one, so unless you go poking around in their roosts, it is not easy to get bitten. Bats do tend to roost in the warm attics of older houses, and sometimes the colonies can build to fairly large numbers, but this is rare. The average suburban home is for the most part bat-free. If some summer night one does happen to get into your house, wait for it to settle, catch it in an old shirt or coat, roll it up, and throw the whole package outdoors. There's no need to kill the poor thing with a broom—the traditional means of ridding the house of errant bats.

There are some forty species of bats throughout the United States and Canada, but unless you catch one and study its markings, it is not an easy mammal to identify.

You can, however, guess at their identity by studying the habitat in which you see them. The hoary bat, the red bat, and the silver-haired bat generally prefer forested habitats, and the brown bats hunt along forest edges and ponds, streams, or lakes. The tiny pipestrelle tends to fly early in the evening and for this reason is probably the bat most often observed over the average back yard.

The most common bat in the United States and Canada is the little brown bat. They roost in caves, buildings, or hollow trees during the day and emerge at night to feed on insects. Little brown bats tend to seek out watery places to do their hunting, and generally they fly late in the evening in darkness, using their exquisite echolocation system to find and catch their food. The other common species you may spot over your back yard is the red bat, although it does not occur in the far West.

When I was about ten years old I used to spend the better part of summer evenings entertaining myself by watching bat flights in my aunt's backyard on the Eastern Shore of Maryland. She had an old decaying barn on her property in which bats (which I now believe were pipestrelles) used to roost. Each evening around dusk I would go out with a handful of stones and wait for the bats to pass over the yard. When they arrived, I would throw a stone into the air, and the bat, assuming it had located a giant moth or some other insect, would swoop down on the stone as it fell, sometimes following it all the way down to within a few yards of the ground. On several occasions I think I remember that the bats caught the stone and carried it for a few seconds before rejecting it, although this may be either my imagination or a poor memory.

In any case, what I do remember is the overall sense of those summer evenings at my aunt's house. The warm air, the rank smell of boxwood, and the delicate flight of the bats tracing a pattern in the red evening sky have served to obliterate all the negative feelings that are generally associated with bats; in fact, I am even partial to them. They are, of course, the only flying mammals, and their flight patterns—the twisting, dives, and aerial acrobatics—to my mind match the flight of swallows and eagles. If you have bats in your back yard, and you have children, do the little ones the favor of giving them a handful of stones and sending them out to play with the bats.

Suburban Snakes

Next to the mosquito, perhaps no single group of animals is more maligned with less cause than the snake. Even the most radical naturalists could perhaps make a case against mosquitoes; they do, in fact, seek you out and bite you. Snakes, by contrast, will do everything in their power to avoid you and will bite only as a last resort; some, such as the hognosed snake, will even feign death before biting. With the single exception of the copperhead, a snake that is slow to bite in any case, the snakes you are likely to find in your yard are not poisonous, and although some will attempt to bite you if you pick them up, most are too small to even break the skin.

I have the bad habit of catching most of the snakes that I find on my land and over the years have been bitten an uncountable number of times. The reason I catch them is to admire the finer beauties that these interesting reptiles exhibit. Next to butterflies, snakes are the most interestingly patterned creatures that you will find in your yard. They come in a variety of sizes, colors, and designs, but in order to observe the sometimes subtle qualities of snake design, you have to observe them close at hand. It is not necessary, however, to catch them and hold them to do this. If you see a snake, and you want to look at it more closely, simply approach it slowly, a step at a time. More often than not the snake will hold its place, flicking its tongue suspiciously (the tongue is a sensory organ in snakes—used to taste the air). Once you are close enough, you can squat down and observe it at leisure.

Garter Snakes

Of all the suburban snakes, perhaps none is encountered more often than the ubiquitous garter snake. If you happen to find an average-sized snake in your yard, no matter where you live, it is likely to be this species. These snakes almost always have three yellow stripes running down their backs, although the background color may vary from green to almost pure black. You may also be able to see a series of dark spots between the yellow stripes. Garter snakes feed on salamanders, frogs, and insects such as grasshoppers, and undoubtedly during their foraging, they will take a number of insect garden pests. As do most snakes, they hunt by stealth, either waiting for or stalking their prey and then striking. They swallow the prey whole, sometimes consuming frogs that seem to be far too large to fit in their mouths. Like many other species, a garter snake's jaws can unhinge, permitting it to swallow large soft-bodied objects such as frogs.

These are feisty little snakes; they will readily attempt to bite you if you pick one up, although the ones I find around the yard are often too small to inflict anything more serious than a few scratches. I am forever moving them out of the way of lawn mowers and scythes, it

Garter Snake

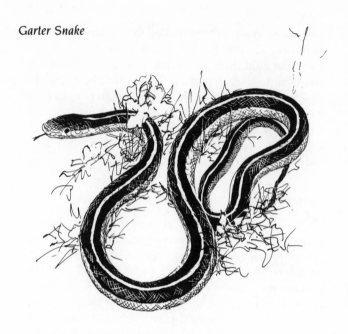

seems, even though I generally get little reward for this act of benevolence; I am regularly bitten throughout the summer. I have come to appreciate, however, the energy with which these snakes attack. They continue to fight in the face of what must seem to them entirely hopeless odds.

Ribbon Snakes

If you live near water, you may spot a striped snake in your yard that, superficially at least, looks very much like a garter snake. The ribbon snake is about two feet long, very slender, and has three bright golden-yellow stripes running down its back. The body is dark brown or black, and the tail is very long and thin, whereas the similarly marked garter snake is somewhat squat and has duller stripes. If you disturb a ribbon snake it will streak off through the grasses like a liquid arrow, and if you are anywhere near water, it will make for it, slip in, and swim away with that beautiful wriggling stroke of water snakes. Ribbon snakes feed mainly on frogs and fish and, like the garter snakes, are feisty and quick to bite. They breed in summer, and the young are born late in the season around August in northern areas.

Smooth Green Snakes

If you keep a section of longer grass on your land, or if after some extended summer vacation your lawn gets out of hand, you may notice, while mowing, a narrow grass-colored snake slither out of harm's way. The green snake, as you might expect given its coloration, prefers a grassy habitat; they can be found in meadows, hayfields, and overgrown lawns. I used to live in a house by the side of a small meadow that I would irregularly mow with a scythe. Inevitably, I would flush one or two of these snakes in the process; they would move off ahead of the blade, climbing and skimming over small tussocks and burrowing into hollows or the cover of the matted grasses, only to reemerge ahead of me. They were sometimes hard to see, and once or twice, I'm sorry to say, I inadvertently did one in. Generally I would catch them and release them again in the cut sections of the meadow.

Green snakes are among the most docile of the native American snakes. I have never been struck at, much less bitten by any of the ones I have handled. They don't seem to mind capture; they will wind themselves through your fingers, and you can "walk" them from hand to hand. If you do find one in your yard, try to catch it; if you happen to have an aversion to snakes, this is a good one to work with to overcome your negative feelings. Quite apart from their docile nature, they are to my mind one of the more beautiful snakes, bright green with colorful jewel-like eyes and pale whitish or yellowish undersides.

The diet of this snake is rather specialized—spiders, smooth caterpillars, and, in the proper season, grasshoppers. Green snakes lay their eggs under warm stones; the young hatch anywhere from a week to three weeks after the eggs are laid, depending, to some extent, on the heat that is absorbed by the stone above the eggs.

Milk Snakes

If you have any outbuildings on your property, a shed or unattached garage for example, you may find a brightly patterned reddish-white snake coiled in a sheltered place in the building at some point during the warmer seasons. The milk snake seems to tend toward human habitations, and although it is more common in rural areas, it is possible to find it in the suburbs and even, on occasion, in the inner city, which is true also of garter snakes. Milk snakes have a blotched pattern of gray to brown or even red patches edged with black. These saddlelike blotches are separated by a gray to white background. The milk snake is quick to bite and can draw blood if it is large enough; but if you want to chance it, it is worth trying to catch one in order to view the beautiful underbelly with its clear checkerboard pattern in white and black. To catch a milk snake, or any snake, grab the animal behind the head either with your hand or by pinning it with a forked stick; hold it lightly by the neck with one hand and support its body with your other hand. It will thrash around for a while, but if you hold it lightly enough it will calm down. Incidentally, be sure to identify the snake *before* you grab it. Milk snakes vaguely resemble copperheads, which also appear in suburban back yards in some sections of the country. Copperheads have a definite hourglass pattern on a copper background, and their heads are flat and diamond-shaped. Fortunately, unlike the milk snake, they are somewhat sluggish and slow to bite.

Ring-necked Snakes

If you have a woodpile, or if you have stored a pile of boards around your property, some day while you are moving things around you may find, at the bottom layer of your stack of wood, a small black snake with a beautiful bright orange-yellow ring around its neck. The ring-necked snake ranges from Canada south to Florida and west to Michigan and is one of the more common local snakes, although it is also one of the more secretive. Although I find them every year in spring while working in the garden, I see them most commonly in early autumn, dead along roadsides. Like many suburban snakes, they seem to seek out the sun-warmed roads late in the season, partly perhaps because of the warmth, although they may also have tracked prey such as small insects there. Ring-necks feed on earthworms, small salamanders, and insects, animals that are not uncommon in the average back yard. They lay their eggs in damp or rotting wood, and the tiny young closely resemble the parents except that they may be somewhat darker. I have lost track of the number of times I have been bitten by this little snake. Inevitably, if you pick one up, it will squirm around and try to nail you. They are too small to inflict any damage, however, and their jaws are too weak or their mouths too small to break the skin. In any case, after a few initial strikes, they always seem to calm down and accept their fate. They tame easily in captivity. There was one at a nature center where I used to work that would accept food from the fingers of schoolchildren.

Other Small Snakes

There are two other small snakes that you may find in the same habitats as the ring-necked—under logs or woodpiles, in other words. The red-bellied snake, as the name implies, has a bright red belly, although in some individuals the color may tend toward orange or even yellow. I usually find them in the garden in spring, under mulch or in or near the compost pile. Red-bellies have brown backs with faint dark stripes. The brown snake, which is even more ubiquitous than the red-bellied or the ring-necked, has light brown undersides and a sprinkling of small black spots along a line of light stripes on its back. They are regularly found beneath logs and rocks, but I have discovered them deep in soil in the garden in spring.

I usually transport all the smaller snakes that I find to my garden, since many of these species feed on insects, insect larvae, and even slugs. One autumn I transplanted a few into my greenhouse to help control the slugs that blossom there in spring, but all of the snakes disappeared in a matter of days—probably into the stone foundation of the house and into the cellar to hibernate.

Local Lizards

Unless you live in a new suburb or anywhere north of the Mason Dixon line, it is likely that at some time you will spot a lizard in your yard. Lizards are notoriously speedy little things and almost impossible to catch, much less to identify. But except for in the extreme South, where several species overlap, you can be fairly certain that you have only one species in your yard. South of the Carolinas in all probability, that species will be the New World chameleon or anole. These are bright little creatures with excellent climbing abilities that can be found everywhere within their range. I used to see them all the time in the middle of the city of Sarasota in Florida, and I also used to see them (I think) in a yard I lived in for a while in Tucson. They are sharp predators that stalk their prey like cats and then at the last minute rush in and seize the unfortunate victim with a quick dart of the tongue.

Another common backyard species, the fence lizard, occurs from New Jersey south to Florida and west to Mexico and Oregon. It is about five to seven inches long, including the tail, and has a gray to brown body etched with V-shaped crossbars. If you spot one and get to observe it for any length of time, you may notice that it periodically goes through a series of pushups—lowering and raising its body quickly. This is a territorial display practiced by the male fence lizard, akin to bird song, although somewhat more prosaic.

Five-lined skinks occur from southern New England to Florida and west to Texas. They have pale stripes that may slowly disappear as the individual lizard ages. Unlike other species of lizards, the skink seems to favor rotting logs, leaf litter, and other cool, moist places. They also inhabit rock piles or trash piles and occasionally can be found in urban areas. This lizard is a great subject of debate, since it is the only one that may occur in New England. There are definite records from the 1930s in Connecticut, for example, as well as a few recent sight-

SUMMER

ings in New York State, but generally official records are few. If you live in the North and you see a "lizard," it is probably a salamander. Salamanders are amphibians and have moist skin and no scales. Lizards are reptiles, have scales, dry skin, and generally favor dry, sunny habitats. The "lizards" you find in your cellar in spring are definitely amphibians (pp. 86–90).

LATE

SUMMER

AUGUST 27 is a magical date for me. On that day, in the region where I live, if the weather is fair, late in the afternoon I can look into the sky and can see sparse flocks of nighthawks wheel by. More than anything else, this event marks—for me at least—the beginning of autumn. It is true that in the human community, the official end of summer—Labor Day—may be a week or two away, and the celestial end, the real end, is still a month off. But somehow, for me, the passage of the nighthawks tells me that the season has finished.

In actuality, the end of summer has been building for weeks. Even in the first few weeks of August, migratory creatures such as barn swallows will begin to congregate on telephone wires and barn ridge poles. Along coastlines, some of the large flights of southbound shore birds will already have passed, and lawns and hayfields have often turned a brown-yellow before the middle of August. Fall webworms have constructed their baglike nests at the end of branches, the fruits are setting on the apple and pear trees, and everywhere the slow winding down of the season has begun.

That is not to say, however, that the end of summer is a depressing season of lengthening shadows, death, and demise. The freshness may be off the bloom, to be

123

sure, but this is also the time of year when a few fresh-
ening weather fronts will pass through, carrying with
them those crystalline late summer days, chilly nights,
and the first sense of the sharpness—the essential good-
ness—of fall. It is to my mind one of the best seasons to
be out of doors. The biting insects are for the most part
gone, the air is often dry, and you can spend full evenings out on the back lawns listening to the chorus of
the katydids and the tree crickets and watching the
shooting stars that appear toward the end of August.

Nightsingers

Toward the end of June or earlier in some parts of the
southeastern states, you may hear, about the time that
the fireflies appear, a faint tinkling in the grass, as if tiny
bells were being sounded by what Gilly Robinson used
to refer to as the fairy musicians. By mid-summer the
tinkling will be joined by a louder chirping, which will
soon be followed by a rasping "scritch," followed by a
dull, musical, pulsating whistle and joined, about the
same time, by an insistent whispering from the trees.
By late August, the nights in the suburbs will be nearly
deafening with the calls of meadow crickets, field crickets, bush and tree katydids, long-horned grasshoppers,
and snowy tree crickets. It is not easy to identify the
songs from books, but there are a number of records on
the market and perhaps in your local library that will
help you sort out the players in the incredible night chorus that will begin toward the end of summer in your
back yard. Better yet, find yourself a good human guide.
Gilly Robinson taught me the calls of local crickets and
katydids in a single August night one year, and I was so
impressed with the diversity of the sounds that I have

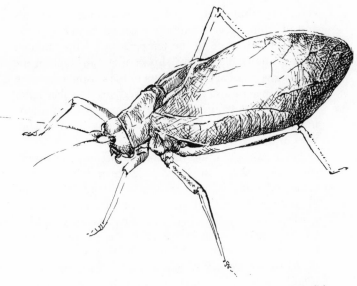

Katydid

never forgotten them. As usual, I found myself wondering why I had never heard them all before.

One of the more interesting and more common night callers is the snowy tree cricket. These slender green insects, which look nothing like the common field crickets you find on your hearth in autumn, often call in unison, and when a large group of them gets together, they more or less overtake the night, overpowering the songs of all but the large katydid. The song is a little like a sustained bell ring, or perhaps a bell-like whistle, and although it is hard to describe, as is often the case in these matters, once you hear it, you will be unable to escape it during late summer.

You can get an approximation of the Fahrenheit temperature by the call of the snowy tree cricket. Simply count the number of throbs or pulses in fifteen seconds and add thirty-seven. Since they are coldblooded, crickets call in response to the temperature of the ambient air; the cooler the air, the slower they call. One of the clear signs of the winding down of the season in autumn is the slowing pulse of these crickets. By October, after the hard frosts begin, you will hear only a few pathetic individuals throbbing out their last notes in the shrubbery of the back yard.

There are a number of species of katydids found throughout the United States, each of which has its characteristic call. Many of these live in old fields, along brushy roadsides, or at the edges of suburban yards and gardens, but the one that is easiest to identify and has lent its name to the entire genus—the so-called true katydid—lives in trees. You cannot help but hear them if you have trees around you—they enunciate their name quite clearly—but whether you will ever see one is questionable. On the other hand, in the house in which I grew up, which was surrounded by large trees, they would regularly land on the window screens and begin calling. They are large green insects that look a little like grasshoppers. The ones that live in fields and brushy edges do not say "katydid." Their calls consist generally of electrical-sounding buzzes, sparks, crackles, or hisses. A record will help you identify them more easily than any verbal description.

One of the last crickets to call in the autumn is the large, black hearth cricket that comes into the house each autumn in rural areas. The presence of this cricket is considered good luck among many country people in Europe, and the Japanese often keep them as pets. They are loud and sometimes disturbing singers, but I take great pleasure in hearing their enduring call from the corner of the living room when the summer fields have long since been devastated by hard frosts and high winds. I like the memory of summer that the call carries with it.

Screech Owls

The insect chorus is not the only sound you may hear in the night in late summer. Sometime in August you may hear an eerie, ghostlike whinny sound out from the trees around your house. If you take a flashlight out and do your best to imitate the call by whistling, you may be able to spot the ghost. The screech owl is a common resident of suburban areas in which there are enough trees for it to nest. It is a small owl, about the size of a large, fat robin, and it is easily attracted by imitations of its call. Sometimes, if you are a good whistler, you can actually bring them to your yard by calling.

Screech owls feed on insects, small birds, and mice and generally nest in holes in trees. They will also take up residence in a special owl nesting box if you set one up on your land. Owl nest boxes, as well as other birdhouses, can often be purchased at local nature centers and garden supply outlets. You can also build them yourself. Plans are generally available at nature centers and are often featured in books on woodworking.

Screech owl nesting begins anywhere from March to mid-April, and you can often see or hear these owls calling during that time of year, but for some reason, I more commonly hear them during late summer. They spend the day roosting in hollows or on branches and, in my experience at least, are rather tame. I once found one in a hole in a tree a few feet from a road. Sometimes it is also possible to find them roosting on the branches of trees—they seem to have a predilection for old apple

Screech Owl

orchards, if you happen to have any in your neighborhood.

The call of the screech owl has perhaps accounted for more ghosts and spirits than any other living creature. Its shivering descending call, echoing through the obscure branches of the night trees, is indeed a somewhat disconcerting sound if you don't know what you are hearing. The former husband of a friend of mine used to hear them in the orchard outside his house when he was little and would lie in bed too terrorized by the call to even tell his parents. It was only later when, as an adult, he identified the call that he came to realize it was not some hideous monster clamoring among the branches of the apple trees.

Not so long ago country people, who knew what they were hearing, used to believe that the call of the screech owl portended a death or some other disaster. Pliny believed that the owl call always betokened heavy news, and the European counterpart of this owl, no doubt, has something to do with the legend of the Irish banshee who always calls out just before a death or misfortune.

Summer Flowers

By mid-summer, in the uncultivated sections of your yard and often in the sort of no man's land between your yard and the road, you can find a new flock of wildflowers blooming. Some of these are hardy perennial weeds that, when they come up in farmers' fields, are considered real pests. On the other hand, anything that will thrive in the uncared-for, untended edges of your property—as most of these flowers do—deserves at least some respect. Look at them more closely and you will see their smaller beauty.

Butter-and-Eggs

LATE SUMMER

Butter-and-Eggs

This aptly named plant grows in hayfields and gardens and unmowed grassy areas. If you even glance at the flowers briefly, you will see the logic of the name. They come in two shades of yellow, one the color of butter, the other the color of scrambled eggs. The leaves look a little like the leaves of flax and account for the other popular name of this plant—toadflax. If you happen to have a section of your land with beds of periwinkle or cypress spurge, you may find the little spires of butter-and-eggs growing up admidst your ground cover. Unfortunately, if you let it go unweeded, you may have, after a while, many butter-and-eggs and very few periwinkles.

Common Mullein

Early in spring, or even during the winter when there is no snow cover, you may notice a rosette of woolly leaves growing in an uncared-for section of your yard. Leave it alone and by mid-summer the rosette will shoot up and produce a tall plant of some three to five feet, with a dense yellow-flowered spike. Once the growing season is over, the spike will endure in the old fields in the landscape until finally the heavy, damp snows of winter will strike it down. Mullein is often seen in old meadows and along roadsides and really is one of the more spectacular weeds of the countryside. It is also one of the more useful, or used to be at any rate. Country people used to dry the leaves and smoke them in order to cure colds or coughs, or sometimes simply steep the leaves in boiling water and breathe in the steam. A friend of mind in Pennsylvania told me that the Amish would commonly use the plant as a cure, but he said that it also had slight narcotic properties and that when he was younger, he and his friends would smoke it in hopes of curing more than simple colds. Mullein is an import from Europe and has a long medicinal history. The Romans recognized its herbal qualities and would also use the spike as a torch. They would dip the long stalk in tallow and light it; the Roman name for the plant is *candelaria*.

Common St. John's-Wort

Another common herbal plant of Europe that has become well established in the back yards and fields of America is the St. John's-wort. The plant was believed to have the power to expel evil spirits, and for centuries in rural Europe, peasants would gather sprigs of St. John's-wort and hang bunches of it over doorways to guard against thunder and to prevent spirits from entering the house. Apparently the remedy worked best if the plants were gathered on the eve of St. John's day, December 27; hence the name for this common plant.

The leaves of St. John's-wort plant do have certain properties, but they are not necessarily beneficial. There is a blistering chemical in the plant that can cause high temperature, rapid pulse, and diarrhea in sheep and cattle if it is consumed in quantity. Since St. John's-wort will creep into a hayfield or any other open area in increasing numbers unless the field is plowed and replanted, it can be a problem in a hay crop. On the other hand, if you are not a farmer, it does have admirably beautiful and abundant five-petaled yellow flowers, each about an inch wide. They appear in leafy clusters at the top of the branched stem. The plant is about three feet tall, and the leaves are somewhat speckled and grow opposite each other.

Chicory

There is a blue flower that you may have unwittingly consumed that may grow in waste places in your yard. Anyone who has ever had coffee in New Orleans may have drunk chicory. It is a common addition to real coffee and is even sold in northern and midwestern supermarkets. Chicory, or coffee cut with chicory, has a distinct dusty flavor that you may or may not enjoy; but

St. John's-wort

if you can find any of these interesting "weeds" around your property, it might be worthwhile digging them up to roast and grind for coffee. Chicory *cafe au lait,* served in the traditional manner with boiled or steamed milk, and accompanied by fresh-baked bread or croissants, makes a good beginning of an autumn morning.

Like many of the plants of disturbed or open areas in the United States, chicory is a native of Europe. The chicory coffee drink originated in France (hence its popularity in New Orleans), and at one point the French would also consume the blanched leaves in salads; in fact, it was cultivated for this purpose for years. To my mind, however, it has had other virtues. It is really one of the more beautiful roadside plants, tall with sky-blue flowers set close to the branching stems. If you can't find chicory in your yard, take a ride through the countryside some day in mid- to late August and watch for the bluest flower in bloom along the roads. The flower is a welcome addition to the national roadside and in my opinion should not be undone by questionable municipal herbicide programs that attempt to eliminate that other common roadside plant, poison ivy.

Chicory is about four feet tall and has branched, hollow stems that turn brown and woody in older plants. The blue flowers are an inch and a half broad, have notched tips, and usually grow in clusters, although only one flower in the group will be open. The leaves look something like the leaves of the dandelion; they are deeply notched or toothed, a little like the teeth of a lion.

Dayflower

Near the garbage can in one house I lived in I discovered a beautiful, although small, flower with a bright yellow

Chicory

pistil and petals so rich, and so deep a blue, that I thought the flower must be some kind of escaped ornamental. It was only after I consulted my flower guides that I learned that it was a dayflower and was considered a useless weed. The beauty or at least the potential beauty of the day-flower has not gone unnoticed by plant propagators, and there are a number of ornamental variations on the basic dayflower theme. They are used as both garden flowers and house plants; the foliage is as attractive as the flow-ers in some ways—rich, succulent leaves that clasp the reclining plant stem at their base.

The leaves of the dayflower grow alternately along the stem, and the flowers appear at the point where the leaves and stem join. They have three petals and are, as I say, a deep blue color. The two upper petals are rounded and larger than the lower one so that viewed head-on the flower looks a little like Mickey Mouse's ears.

Common Nightshade

There is one other deep blue or purple flower with a yellow center that you may find blooming at the edges of your yard in summer. Common nightshade has the same lush quality to its flowers that the smaller day-flower has. Late in the season it will produce a crop of delicious-looking black berries that are toxic in the early stages of development. There are about thirty species of plants in this family in the United States and Canada, and most of them provide an abundance of food for wildlife. Cardinals, catbirds, sparrows, mockingbirds, goldfinches, and other local suburban birds feed on the berries, as do raccoons, skunks, mice, and pocket gophers; it is really one of the more useful plant families as far as wildlife is concerned. Although flowers in the nightshade family are generally blue or purple, in some species the flower can be white. One of the more common characteristics of these flowers are the bright yellow, beaklike anthers (the part of the flower where the pollen develops). The yellow anthers protrude from the center of the five petals and make a good field mark. The petals curve back slightly toward the plant, and the flowers appear in clusters at the end of stalks.

Jewel-weed

If you have any semishaded damp spots on your property, you may be able to find a few jewel-weed plants growing there. The plant is about three feet high and has almost fragile, lance-shaped leaves and bright yellow-lipped flowers that vaguely resemble tiny trumpets. There are two certain identification tests for jewel-weed. If you submerge the leaves in water, they will take on a silvery sheen, and once the seeds have set, if you even so much as breathe on the seed pod, or look at it in the wrong way, it seems, it will quiver and shoot out its seeds, leaving a curly springlike appendage in their place. This shooting habit, not an uncommon practice among certain plant species, gives jewel-weed its other common name—touch-me-not.

The foliage of jewel-weed is very tender and is reported to make a good potherb. It may also serve as a field remedy to poison ivy and nettle stings. If you brush a nettle, grab a handful of jewel-weed leaves and rub them on the spot and you will not experience the stinging itch from the nettle. Used in this manner, supposedly the plant will also prevent poison ivy rashes, although I have never trusted this bit of folklore enough to test the premise.

LATE SUMMER

Grass

Of all the weeds that appear in your back yard during the growing season, none is perhaps more despised, more discriminated against, and the subject of more eradication programs than the wild grasses. Basically grass grows in two different forms, those species that form a deep, impenetrable mat of roots and soil known as sod, and those that sprout in small clumps or bunches. Unless you have religiously herbicided, fertilized, and clipped your lawn on a regular schedule, you will probably be able to spot both types no more than a few feet from your back door. The more desirable of the two groups are the fescues and the bluegrasses, which are commonly sold as lawn grass and which form sod and tend to resist invasion from other species of plants. By contrast, many of the enemies of groundskeepers fall into the category of bunch grasses; you will see little clumps of these coming up amidst the greensward of your lawn. Of the latter group, perhaps the most infamous is crab grass, which is one of the more persistent weed grasses of suburban lawns. Crab grasses, which are annual grasses, produce a large quantity of seeds that are eaten by a large number of species of birds and mammals, including juncos, sparrows, doves, rabbits, and mice. Crab grasses are also resistant to drought and in dry periods during late summer may remain green, whereas other species of grass, without water, will turn a depressing, dead-looking brown.

Other wild species of annual grass and bunch grasses may appear in your lawn during the summer; orchard grass, barnyard grass, foxtail, canary grass, and redtop may move into your lawn if you let it go for any length of time. You have but to visit the yard of an abandoned house to see what would happen to your lawn if you weren't there to mow it and weed it every week or so.

LATE SUMMER

It is perhaps worthwhile saying something here about your lawn; it is, after all, or has become, the most common ecosystem in the suburban American landscape in certain sections of the country. The concept of the lawn, a stretch of grass-covered, closely mown land, is an English invention, and in most parts of the United States and Canada (and in fact in most parts of England as well) it is essentially a transitional and artificially maintained ecosystem. If you stop tending to your lawn, the area will attempt to return to the climax condition that exists in wild areas around your neighborhood—which in most parts of the country is forest. Even with constant maintenance, local weeds and perennial plants will attempt to establish themselves. Most of these so-called weed species are more or less pioneer plants—small trees, shrubs, and herbaceous plants that will create the conditions necessary for the growth of the common trees in your region—either hardwoods or, in some areas of the North and South, pine trees. This transitional state between greensward and forest is known technically as an early seral stage and is recognized by ecologists as one of the more diverse upland ecosystems known. If you want to attract wildlife to your property, if you want to see wildflowers on your land, small shrubs, foxes, mice, woodchucks, skunks, possums, songbirds, quail, pheasants, frogs, and snakes, simply stop mowing your lawn for a few years. When, after ten or fifteen years, it is clear that your land is becoming a young forest, you can cut it all down, plow it, till it, seed it, and start all over again.

The alternative to this is a constant nurturing of the perennial grasses that were seeded on your grounds when your house was built. Nowhere have I heard a better explication of the needs that this artificial habitat requires than from a grizzled old groundskeeper on an estate near Salisbury, England. A friend with whom I was traveling asked the old gardener how he kept such a perfectly smooth, ruglike greensward. "Well, mum," he answered, "you seed it, and you roll it, and you clip it, and you seed it, and you roll it, and you clip it, and you do that for maybe four hundred years and you'll have a lawn such as you see before you."

Given the constraints of mortality, not to mention the mobile tendencies of suburban Americans, it is perhaps better to put away your lawn mower for the rest of your life. Your local wildlife will appreciate the change.

Insect Pests

One of the best places to find insects in your back yard, unfortunately, is in the middle of your garden. As soon as the first pea shoots appear or the first radishes, as soon as you set out your broccoli, battalions of crop-consuming enemies invade, as if from nowhere, to compete with you for the harvest. You may go for years in your yard without a garden and never see a potato bug. But if one year you dare to plant even a single row of potatoes, as surely as the day follows the night, one will appear. If you are interested in insects and don't care about food, you might try planting a small garden just to see what will show up. The diversity and the range of color, shape, and feeding habits are marvelous to behold. If they weren't attempting to eat the same plants as we are, we might be better able to admire them for their beauty.

Potato Bugs

The aforementioned potato bug ranks as one of the more splendid looking pests in the vegetable garden. The adults

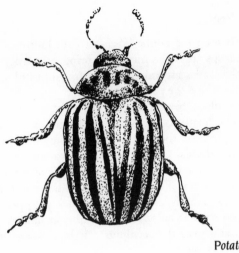

Potato Bug

are about a half-inch long and are handsomely striped with yellow and black lines. They hibernate through the winter and then emerge in spring to lay their eggs on the underside of the leaves of potatoes, tomatoes, and other garden crops. In contrast to the adults, the larvae that hatch from these eggs are hideous, fat-bodied, pink things that sluggishly feed on plant foliage for the next two or three weeks. The larvae then pupate, adults emerge, and the cycle begins again. I have found that the best control for these pests is to watch carefully for the golden eggs and then scrape them off before the cycle even gets under way. Barring that, you might try hand-picking the adults, always one of the best alternatives to pesticides in the smaller garden.

LATE SUMMER

Flea Beetles

Shortly after the young leaves of your radishes or other leafy crops appear in the early spring, you might notice that the leaves are riddled with tiny shot holes. Watch the soil around the plants carefully and you will see hordes of tiny black beetles around the stem or even on the leaves of the plants. These are flea beetles, and generally, unless there are too many of them, they may be harmless little things. On the other hand, a large infestation of them may wipe out a row or two of radishes or spinach, and even if it doesn't, the small holes in the leaves may make it easier for disease to attack your plants. The best control is to cultivate thoroughly around the young plants and give the seedlings a light dusting of wood ashes every once in a while.

Cutworms

One of the greatest disappointments of the home gardener is to wait expectantly for two weeks or so for the beans to sprout, or to set out a row of carefully nurtured broccoli seedlings, and then find some morning that during the night the whole row has been laid low—not eaten, but simply clipped off at the stem. This act of seemingly wanton vandalism is wrought by the cutworm, the larva of a rather undistinguished moth. The worms lie curled in the soil during the day—you may often see them when you are cultivating—but at night emerge to clip the vegetable crops. Once the larvae have grown up, they will burrow deep in the soil and pupate, and the brown-patterned adult moths will appear in a few weeks.

The best way to protect seedlings from cutworms is to construct little collars for your plants. The cutworm season doesn't last more than three or four weeks, and if your plants can grow a thick enough stem, the larvae will be unable to do any damage. Another method of control is to cultivate thoroughly in the autumn to destroy the eggs and any pupae that are lying dormant in the soil.

Stalk Borers

The worst enemy of my garden, the singular insect with no redeeming qualities that I can discover, is the stalk borer. I had no problem with these insidious creatures when I first put in my garden. But over the years their numbers slowly increased until finally one year there was not a single stemmed plant, it seemed, that could avoid their devastation. The first sign that you have a stalk borer problem is a sick-looking plant with wilted leaves. Check the stem carefully and you will find a tiny hole, often surrounded by the whitish residue of the worm's borings. Garden books will tell you that it is possible to slit the stem and extract the larva with little harm to the plant, but I have never had much success with this method; for one thing, in their heyday, there were too many borers to dig out. Systemic pesticides supposedly control borers on ornamentals, but the few that are on sale are often highly toxic and are not recommended for food crops. In any case, most of the pesticides are sold as preventatives—once you have a borer problem, they are difficult to eradicate.

The worm that does all the damage is a brownish thing with black dots. There are a number of species, and related common borers such as the cornstalk borer may leave your corn patch to work over other crops. The worms are the larvae of a brown moth with white wing spots that lays its eggs on nearby grasses or weeds. The eggs hatch in spring, and the young larvae move toward the larder of the garden. I have heard that one of the better preventative measures for this pest is to mow a close-cropped swathe of grass around your garden to keep the moths from laying their eggs near your food crops.

Tomato Hornworms

Another disappointing garden experience is to find that the leaves of your tomato plants are slowly disappearing, chunk by chunk. Search as you will, you cannot find the cause, until finally, one day, with half the plants destroyed and the potential harvest sadly diminished, you will see an immense three- to four-inch green caterpillar sluggishly moving along the stem of a plant or lying still among the leaves.

Damaging though it is, the tomato hornworm is one of the more interesting pests in the home garden. For one thing, the caterpillars are handsome devils, and the adults, known as hawk moths, are large, beautiful insects with brightly patterned hind wings that feed on the nectar of deep-throated flowers. The moths hover in front of the flower as they feed and are often mistaken for hummingbirds, and in fact they are almost as large, about five inches in length generally.

I have learned how to spot the handiwork of hawk moth larvae—the great bite-size chunks from the leaves—and once I notice the damage, I diligently search the plant or the whole patch if necessary until I find the culprit. There are never so many hornworms as to prevent hand-picking in the small garden. The other control is to watch for the pupa in the soil. It is a large brown cigar-shaped tube about two inches in length. I always find them while I am turning the soil in spring.

LATE SUMMER

Leaf Hoppers

One of the more significant cases of justice (or injustice) occurred in the garden of an old leftist friend of mine. City-bred by nature, with years of radical politics behind him and struggling with an increasing case of paranoia, he deserted political life altogether and moved to the country to cultivate his own garden. In order to help himself through the struggle of change, carefully concealed behind his tomatoes and his corn he planted a small patch of marijuana for personal use. Things went well that summer in his garden; there were very few pests, and it looked like a good harvest was in store. But he began to notice that the leaves of his marijuana plants were curling sadly, only to die and drop off. Inspecting the plants carefully, he found that they were covered with small bright insects handsomely patterned in blue and red, and looking for all the world like tiny American flags. My friend was still sane enough to know it was coincidence, but the thought did cross his mind that these decidedly American insects were part of some nasty harassment plotted by the CIA or the FBI.

The insects that consumed my friend's plants were red-banded leaf hoppers, and although hardly agents of the government, they do wreak havoc among certain vegetable and farm crops. They are only one of many leaf hopper species, a group that generally feeds by sucking the sap from plants. A few leaf hoppers will not cause much of a problem, but when there are too many, the leaves will whither and curl. It is believed that the leaf hoppers excrete a plant toxin as they feed. They are known to spread plant viruses, and of course they weaken the plant by sucking out the life juices. They are difficult to control except with pesticides, and left to their own devices, the populations of these insects can build to huge numbers.

LATE SUMMER

Allies in the Garden

Although your garden will attract any number of insect pests that you never knew existed in your area, it will attract predators of all types as well. Through careful management—that is, without resorting to the indiscriminate use of pesticides—it is possible to strike an ecological balance in your garden in which the predators hold control over the crop consumers.

Excluding rabbits, woodchucks, and some species of birds, the prime enemies of your garden are insects, and it is perhaps somewhat comforting to know that arrayed against this single class are mammals, birds, reptiles, amphibians, arachnids, and predatory insects. One of the better-known creatures in this vigilant army is the humble toad. As I have pointed out elsewhere (see page 42), nightly this amphibian emerges to patrol the garden rows and will consume many times its weight in pest species. The trick to attracting toads is to provide hiding places for them. A half-buried jar, a propped-up board, or even well-loosened soil will offer these amphibians a cool, protected place to spend the day. You can also increase the toad population by transporting the ones that you find elsewhere in your yard to the garden. Green snakes, garter snakes, red-bellied snakes, and brown snakes will feed on a variety of insect pests that live in the soil and on the plants themselves, and surrounding the garden in webs, and in small burrows or patrolling along the rows are a diverse number of arachnids who, if unharmed by indiscriminate pest-control methods, will be attracted to your garden specifically because there are pests there.

In the spring and again in the fall, skunks will dig up the grubs of many insect pests, such as the hawk moth larva and the cutworms, and shrews and moles will also feed on soil-dwelling grubs and adults. Swallows and flycatchers will snap up flying insects, including pests such as the cabbage butterfly and the adult stage of the stalk borer. But as far as birds are concerned, perhaps the greatest friend to the garden is the unpopular starling. The starling has an inordinate fondness for cutworms, and I have seen small flocks of them descend on my garden and diligently waddle up and down the rows plucking off other pest insects from the plants and from off the ground.

Finally, the greatest bane to insect pests are other insects. Most famous of these is probably the praying mantis. If you find the egg case of this insect during the winter months, you might transport it to the garden. The eggs will hatch during the warmer weather—about the time that your garden pests are at their zenith—and the voracious young will go to work as soon as they emerge. The adult, which can be recognized by its large forelegs, held more often than not in the posture of prayer, feeds at leisure on its prey, holding it crosswise as if it were an ear of corn.

The other favorite garden pest control is the handsomely marked ladybug, which can be recognized by its mandolin-shaped body marked with black dots on a red background. Both the adults and larvae of these insects feed on aphids, which can be a major pest in some gardens and, if they get out of control, can wipe out crops in a greenhouse. The popularity of ladybugs has a long history. They were recognized as allies of the farmers and gardeners as far back as the Middle Ages; the fact that they were dedicated to the Virgin Mary and were generally known as the beetles of Our Lady is perhaps a measure of the respect that European peasants felt for this insect.

Apart from these well-known predatory insects, there are other, less-recognized allies: tachinid flies, which parasitize squash bugs; brachonid wasps, which parasitize tomato hornworms; and a variety of similar predators, such as the ambush bug, which chases down smaller insects. Unfortunately, many of these useful predators are killed by the same insecticides that are applied to control the pest species, and since they are lower down on the food chain and there are more of them, the pests will recover much more readily than will the predators.

Orange Garden Spiders

When I first came to the house in which I now live there was, in back of the house in the place where a lawn would normally be, a tangle of long grass, blackberries, poison ivy, and various escaped perennials. I moved into the house in late August and early in the morning of the first day began to explore this wild meadow. It was one of those classic summer mornings, clear with heavy dew on the grasses, and the air was redolent of the rich morning smell of late summer. Not ten yards from the back door I came across the glassy wheel of a spider's web, each line and silken thread hung with jewel-like dew drops that sparkled in the light. Before I completed the exploration, I had counted eight of these webs, each vying with the other for brilliance. In subsequent months, and during the following spring, I cleared most of the meadow and in the process also cleared away the spiders. By the next autumn I realized my mistake and the following summer allowed some of the tangle to return. With the blackberries and the long grasses came the orange garden spiders and their wondrous webs.

The spider that weaves the dew-silvered webs is a member of the genus *Argiope*. Females are about one inch long, males are shorter, and both the male and the

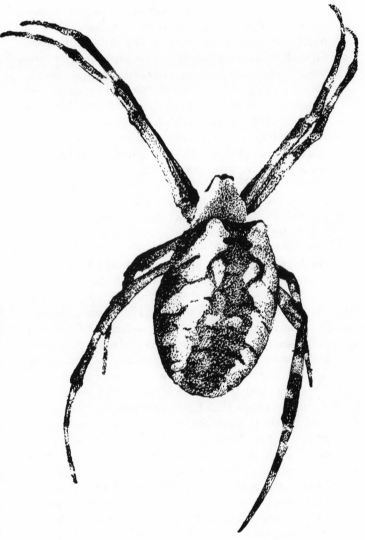

Garden Spider

female are brightly patterned with orange or yellow spots and stripes that form a band along both sides. They are highly conspicuous and certainly one of the more colorful spiders in North America. They are also fairly common; if you have an older perennial garden or an area thickly planted with low shrubs or a wild section of your property, you are likely to find one of these. Watch for them especially in the early mornings when the webs are hung with dew; they are easiest to find then.

If you touch one of the webs lightly, the spider may shake the entire structure, though why she does this is not known. If by chance you crash through the web, or touch it too roughly, the spider will drop from its perch and hide in the plants at the base of the web.

Construction of the web takes place generally at night and is a fairly involved process. The spider begins by climbing down one support system and up another to string an irregular five- or six-sided framework about one foot across. It then drops a line down the middle to the bottom, returns to the center and fastens another line, climbs down the first line and along the framework, attaches another line at an angle to the center line, and returns to the center. It continues this process until it has made a wheel-like web with some twenty spokes. The spider then goes to the center and begins to weave a spiral between the spokes attaching the line to each spoke in the process. She returns to the framework and begins a spiral from the outside. When the orb is finished, she weaves down the center, a ladderlike ribbon of white thread known popularly as the winding stair. This structure may strengthen the web or may simply be ornamentation. In any case, with the web completed, the orb weaver takes up a position near the center and waits for some unsuspecting insect to fly or jump into her net.

FALL

IF YOU LIVE in a colder region, the appearance of the first frost on your property may be a more momentous event than almost any other natural occurrence; more so even than the first snow, or the appearance of the first snowdrops in spring. Some morning (early frosts inevitably occur at night) you will wake up to find that everything you have known and cherished and nurtured through the warm, languorous days of summer is coated with a rime of white crystal. By the end of the day, after the sun has reached the plants, you will see that the more tender annuals, and not a few of your perennials, will have been transformed from a lush, flowering green to a deathlike black. Except perhaps for major snowstorms, or hurricanes or tornadoes, there is nothing that can transform your yard so dramatically and so precipitously.

Most of the damage from frost will occur on plants that have been imported from warmer climates—the squashes, the beans, and the marigolds. But this is by no means the end of the season for many species of native plants. Although the landscape may be stripped down by degrees, the rains of autumn often bring out a lushness in the plant world that is equaled only by spring. The dry, dusty look of August takes on a richer hue, the grasses on suburban lawns green up once more, and many species of ornamental plants and wild plants, including chrysanthemums, asters, and goldenrods, go into flower. Mushrooms appear overnight in fields, woods, and lawns; the nut and fruit crop ripens to its fullest; and, in a flip side of spring, the full force of summer comes to fruition.

And yet it is all doomed. Slowly, as the season progresses, the flowers blossom and fade, the mushrooms shed their spores and shrivel, the leaves fall from the trees, and all the world will turn a somber lion brown, the pervasive color of November.

Life in the Sky

Even if you have only a few square yards of grass behind the kitchen door for a back yard, if you happen to have a view of the sky, then you have access to what is in effect the greatest wilderness of all. During the day, the sky provides an ever-changing panoply of colors, cloud forms, moods, and shapes. It also contains a veritable sea of living creatures. I have a friend who, after being laid off from his job, decided to more or less desert the world for a while. He was given a cabin on a clear hill in southern Vermont, and in spite of the fact that he had to walk a mile to get water and had no electricity and few other conveniences, he spent the better part of the year there thinking things over, reading books, and going for nature walks in the surrounding hills. One of the revelations that came to him there was the amount of life that packs itself into a square cubic yard of the atmosphere. This is a phenomenon that came to him first—quite understandably—during the height of early summer, when insect hatchings are at their peak. He began to notice one day in June that the things were forever crossing his view—gnats, bees, spiderlings paying themselves out on threads of webs, butterflies, songbirds, hawks overhead, bits of fluff from seeds, and drifting clouds of mayflies and midges. He became so conscious of the life in the air that he began to notice the subtleties of the aerial dynamics, could see layerings of life, certain species of insects at one level, for example, certain species of birds at another, and so on. It was only during the depths of winter that he said the crowd of life in the sky diminished.

This same Vermont sky, with its rich baggage of life, exists over the suburbs of North America. In some sections, the lower layers—that is, the area in which the woods-dwelling insects and small songbirds would be found—may not be as populated as the sky over Vermont; but the upper regions are filled with passing hawks and turkey vultures, drifting spiderlings, and seed fluff.

Ironically, at no time is this phenomenon of life in the sky more apparent than at night in autumn. Many species of songbirds and shorebirds migrate in darkness, and since most fly at heights that are measured in thousands of feet, they are visible over city and suburb alike. The time to watch them is when the moon is full. This is one of those events that you can be certain of experiencing if you pick your dates properly. The time of the month varies from region to region, but if you check with your local nature center or science center, you can find out when the autumn migration is taking place. Check to see when the moon is at least half-full during this migration period, wait for a clear night, and then go out to your back yard with a chair and a pair of binoculars. Make yourself comfortable (I have found that turning the chair around and resting your arms on the back makes watching easier) and focus your glasses on the moon. In due time, you will see the darting forms of birds passing. If you live along the coast, these may be shorebirds—which usually migrate earlier than songbirds, from mid-summer through mid-October—but if you live inland, the birds you see will probably be thrushes and sparrows and the like. If you live in a quiet neighborhood away from highways and traffic, you may hear the migrants as well as see them. Not all species of birds fly at such great heights, and if you listen carefully while you are watching the moon, periodically you will hear the tiny cheeps and chirps of land birds passing overhead in the dark.

To my mind, this night passage of birds—an event that takes place each year unbeknownst to perhaps 90 percent of the human population and yet is accessible to almost everyone—is one of the greatest seasonal events in the natural world. There is something very comforting about the fact that, in spite of war, pollution, crime in the streets, and all the other ills that affect the human community, the sheer force of the migratory drive is still working well and the world is all right in the end.

Hawk Migration

There is another migration that takes place each year in autumn, this one far better recognized than the night passage of songbirds and shorebirds. From early September through mid-November vast numbers of hawks and eagles move down the great ridges of mountains and hills of the eastern and western United States. Generally these predatory birds are channeled past certain points, and if the weather conditions are right, they may form concentrations that number in the thousands. On one day, for example, the better part of the entire eastern population of broad-winged hawks may be observed.

Hawk Mountain in Pennsylvania is perhaps the most famous hawk-watching spot in the East; but there are many others throughout the United States, the greater portion of them perhaps yet to be discovered.

It is true that in order to see these vast concentrations, you must leave the confines of your back yard, but it is also possible to see individual hawks passing overhead during the autumn from any back yard with a view of the sky. On a clear Saturday in fall, when the wind is in the northwest—not an uncommon weather condition in autumn—check the sky periodically while you are out raking leaves. There is a strong possibility that you will see at least one or two hawks pass over your yard. And if you are observant and live in a good area, you may count as many as a hundred or so.

Over the past few years I have gotten into the habit of spending Saturday or Sunday afternoons on the roof of my back porch. I take a pot of tea, climb a ladder I have built up the side of the house to my perch, and spend a few hours there, watching the sky, sipping tea, and daydreaming. I don't happen to live in a very good area for hawk watching; all the valleys and ridges run the wrong way. But on a single afternoon in early September I spotted fourteen broad-winged hawks. I have seen any number of red-tailed hawks, sharp-shinned, and Cooper's hawks, as well as a few ospreys. I once saw a bald eagle from my perch, and one afternoon I spotted a golden eagle overhead, something of a rarity where I live.

Red-tailed Hawks

If you spend any amount of time watching the autumn sky in late October, you will in all likelihood see at least one red-tailed hawk pass over your house. They are easy to identify, especially on clear, sunny days. The dull red on the top of the tail can be spotted whenever the hawk dips slightly or adjusts its flight, and if you look carefully, the red often shows through the tail when the light is strong enough. Watch also for the light-colored breast and the streaking on the belly of the bird. You don't necessarily need binoculars to identify this hawk. For one thing, it is one of the more common species, and once you learn to identify the general shape, you can be fairly certain—in the East, at any rate—that a large, chunky hawk with wide or fat wings and a short tail is a red-tail. Falcons have slim wings and a darting flight, while Cooper's hawks and sharp-shinned hawks have longer tails and tend to flap their wings more than the other common hawks.

I once had an experience with a red-tailed hawk that was to me a graphic demonstration of the incredible eyesight these birds possess. There was a red-tail at a nature center where I once worked, a handsome bird that had broken its right wing and was doomed to spend the rest of its life in a large outdoor cage. Part of my job was to feed this bird every day, and in the course of a few months it got to know me fairly well. One day I noticed that it was crouching in its cage cocking its head to the sky and calling desperately. I looked up but could see nothing but the arc of the October sky, free of clouds. The hawk continued its behavior and had no interest in the food I was offering it. Thinking I must be missing something, I went inside, got my binoculars, and searched the sky. Finally I found the object of its interest. Through the high-powered glasses I located two tiny specks circling in a gyre—both invisible to my naked eye. I watched them for a while and was finally able to identify them as red-tails. These birds can spot tiny mice and even well-camouflaged frogs and snakes from great heights.

Broad-winged Hawks

Another common migratory hawk is the chunky, crow-sized broad-wing. Like red-shouldered hawks, these birds have a banded tail and a definite soaring habit, but they are much smaller. Broad-wings begin their migration in mid-September and by the end of the month may build to huge numbers. They often migrate in soaring flocks, so if you see one overhead, look for others. As many as 1,500 may be counted in a single day in the right area.

Broad-winged hawks nest in suburban areas; one year a pair constructed a nest and raised young a hundred yards beyond my office window at the Massachusetts Audubon Society in Lincoln, Massachusetts. The avid hawkwatchers at the society set up a telescope and focused it on the nest, and periodically throughout the day, people on their way to the coffee machine would glance through the scope, mark down the time on a sheet of paper, and write a few comments on the behavior of the hawks. That same year a broad-winged hawk nested in an oak tree about twenty yards into the woods beyond the little meadow to the north of my house. The hawk had to cross the meadow whenever it returned to the nest from the south, west, or east, and so I often got a good view of it as it brought food for its young. Although this nest was not visible, in some ways I learned as much from this particular nester as from the closer one at the Lincoln office. The main thing was that I was able to verify the fact that broad-winged hawks eat a lot of snakes. It seemed to me, although I kept no formal records of the food, that with every other trip to the nest,

Snow Geese

the adults carried a dangling snake to their young—most likely a garter snake.

Geese

One of the other natural phenomena you may be able to see or hear in the sky during autumn is the passage of southbound flocks of wild geese. It is somehow a deeply comforting experience to wake some night and hear, raining out of the night sky beyond the bedroom window, the high bark of a large flock of Canada geese. It can be heard in the most crowded suburbs, even in cities, and as with the passage of smaller birds, no matter how complex your life may be, no matter how crowded with schedules, meetings, school problems, child problems, marital problems, and all the other ills in the long litany of suburban woes, the bark of passing geese belies a deeper order to things. Life goes on, and will go on, no matter what you do.

By day, from the confines of the back yard, you may also be able to see the flocks, even if you live far inland. I once lived in a small clearing in the middle of a vast state forest, and in spite of my limited view of the sky, each season in spring and fall I could see geese going over. They would pass sometimes in huge squadrons, flying so high that they were barely visible to the naked eye. I remember one day in April hearing what I thought to be a huge pack of beagles coursing through the deep woods. The sound came and went on the gentle winds, and after some analysis and not a little searching, I finally saw them—an immense flock of snow geese moving rank on rank above the small clearing, headed, as I later calculated, for their breeding grounds on Mackenzie Bay. Even at great heights, the two common species of geese in the United States and Canada, the snow goose and the Canada goose, can be distinguished. Canada geese fly in the standard goose chevron formation, the long skeins or V's that are depicted in so many waterfowl paintings. Snow geese tend to fly in a broad curving front or wave-shaped formation. "Wavies" is a common waterman's term for these beautiful white geese.

The wavies passed over my clearing in the forest on April 12. The next year as the twelfth approached I started listening for them again and watching the sky. The eleventh passed with no sign, the twelfth was cold and cloudy, and then on the morning of the thirteenth, under a clear blue sky, I heard them coming. There were so many, it took the flocks almost fifteen minutes to go by. The next year they went over on the tenth. And although I had moved by the following year, on the tenth again, in Concord, Massachusetts, a huge flock settled on the marshes of the Concord River. Say what you will about the world; there is an order of sorts.

Flickers

There is one bird that may pass through your yard in autumn and may stand out from the confusing array of small, nondescript birds that flit through your hedges and shrubs during the migration season. The flicker is one of the few migratory woodpeckers. It can be recognized by the black mustache markings near its bill (in males and young females) and its black neckband. It is also one of the easier birds to recognize in flight: it has a wonderful dipping, roller-coaster flying pattern that is pretty much unmistakable and reveals the bird's brilliant white rump patch. In spite of the fact that it is a member of the woodpecker family, one of the favorite foods of the flicker is the ground-dwelling ant. You will often see flickers hunting ants on the lawn, their heads tilted off to one side to get a better view of the action.

Flickers migrate in early fall and for some reason seem to have a harder trip than many other species. If you are a walker or a jogger, in late September and early October you may begin to notice large numbers of dead flickers along back roads and suburban streets. If you do happen to find a fresh specimen, pick it up and take a good look at it. The rich browns, the intricate patterns of the feathers, and the red patch on the heads of the males should help overcome any revulsion you may feel at the thought of handling dead birds. (If you pick up a freshly-killed bird of any species, you may notice a number of tiny, light-colored insects crawling about on your hand. These are the feather lice that inhabit virtually all species of birds. Don't worry about them; since you don't have feathers, they will soon leave you, even if you don't brush all of them off.)

There are two distinct species of flicker. East of the Mississippi watch for the yellow-shafted flicker; in the West look for the red-shafted. The underside of the tail and wings are red in the red-shafted, yellow in the yellow-shafted.

I once had a graphic demonstration of the extensive and determined nature of bird migration, in which flickers were the main players. A few years ago, during the height of the fall migration, I spent a week on a fishing boat on George's Bank, 100 miles off the coast of Massachusetts. As is often the case on the Bank, there was some nasty weather at the beginning of the week that must have confused the migratory birds. For days after the weather cleared, I could look out over the wilderness of the Atlantic and see flickers roller-coasting just above the crests of the waves, 100 miles off-course but headed south nonetheless with blind determination.

Mammals

There are a few mammals abroad in summer, such as the woodchuck, that disappear into hibernation fairly early in the autumn. But partly because of the quantity of fruits and nuts, autumn brings on a sort of mad scramble among certain common rodents, such as mice and squirrels. None of the squirrels that you see in your yard is a true hibernator; all will remain active through-out the winter. But in order to survive the spare season, they have to store up as much food in their larders as they can—hence the activity. The foraging of squirrels of autumn is a well-known phenomenon, even among schoolchildren (it was a major part of my second-grade curriculum, as I remember); but the activities of other mammals in fall—less popular ones, such as skunks—remain untaught and perhaps ill-understood.

Deer Mice

The first frosts always seem to generate a lot of activity among birds and mammals. I often notice that local flocks of Canada geese become more active on or around the days of the first frost, and although it may be pure imagination on my part, it seems to me that the red and the gray squirrels begin foraging with more intensity. As in the human community, the colder air seems to generate energy among the denizens of the nearby wil-derness areas beyond the back door.

One of the most remarkable of these autumnal events in an annoying sort of way is the small migrations of a

Deer Mouse

creature known commonly as the white-footed mouse, or deer mouse. There are several species in this general group, including the canyon mouse and the California mouse; but of these, the most widely distributed is the deer mouse. These interesting little creatures with bright black eyes range from Maine to California and may be found in open areas—in the Midwest, for example—and in wooded areas in the East and far West. They also vary greatly in coloration. Some of them may be quite gray, or gray brown, and some may be a deep reddish brown. The distinguishing characteristic of this mouse is its tail, which is divided into two colors, dark above, white below.

Deer mice generally are a ground-dwelling species, although they will climb trees and will nest in the oddest sort of places. I have found nests of these mice in wood-piles, in the walls of chicken coops, in discarded heating ducts, in birds' nests, house and barn walls, tree hollows, and almost any place else that is sheltered. The nest looks very much like a ball of dry grass or feathers and twigs and, unless you know what to look for, will be overlooked by your average back-yard explorer. But, as with many of the things in this book, once you learn to spot them, you will begin to see them all over, even in the most urbanized suburbs. I once found a nest in the air conditioner of a small industry. All the mouse really needs for habitat is a small stretch of woodland.

If you carefully dissect a mouse nest you will find more often than not remnants of the food of the deer mouse, bits of nutshell, grass seeds, and the seeds of herbaceous plants. They also feed on roots and tubers, although the remains of these are not often found in the nest. Acorns, blueberries, knotweeds, and maple seeds seem to rank fairly high on the menu of the deer mouse, although in western areas they appear to eat a lot of cedar and pine.

Actually, before you get a chance to inspect the nest, you may be surprised by the inhabitant. Any number of times I have started to pull apart what I assumed was an abandoned nest only to have the mother mouse burst out of the ball of grass and disappear, sometimes followed by her young, sometimes deserting them altogether. In the latter case, you will find in the very center of the rounded tangle a hollow filled with squirming pink babies—one of the favorite foods of the milk snake and other smaller snakes.

Around the time of the first frosts, like any sensible creature, these mice tend to seek out warm sites and good supplies of food. If you live in or near woods, it is likely that at least one family of these mice will set up quarters in the walls of your house. The house mouse, which may also be found in your walls, is a gray, chunkier species that is not indigenous to this country. Mice tend to be noisy at night (undoubtedly they account for a number of ghosts or poltergeists), and they can be somewhat brazen—I once watched one attempt to carry off a walnut that was at least half its size, and my presence and the fact that the nut belonged to me did not seem to deter it in any way.

Unless the populations get out of hand—not an uncommon situation—I always allow the innocent deer mice to share the goods. It is, after all, a cold world, and they always leave for the fields and woods when the weather gets better.

Skunks

Each year around the middle of September I am forced to do battle with skunks. They come in waves onto my property, in certain years in full battalions, in other years in small squads of guerrillas; but they come unerringly—there is something about my land that attracts them. During the late summer and early fall young skunks, born in the spring, are out searching for new territory and new dens for winter. Because the house I live in is old and has an all but unrepairable stone foundation with a mere crawl space under most of the house, the place seems to hold an irresistible attraction for these interesting and intelligent members of the weasel family. They appear in my cellar with annoying regularity; they break into my greenhouse through the crawl spaces under the house, and one year one even managed to work its way into a cupboard in the kitchen. I would tolerate their presence except for the fact that they have the habit of fighting under my window at four in the morning, and invariably, at some point during the autumn, one of them will spray under the house or along the foundation, causing the place to reek on damp days for weeks afterward.

But while they are a nuisance, I begrudgingly welcome them. For one thing, they do a good job of cleansing the garden of pesky grubs; the diet of the three common species of skunk in the United States consists primarily of insects, although they will also consume other beneficial insect predators, such as frogs, mice, and snakes. Skunks also feed on a certain amount of plant material, mainly fruits and berries such as grapes, blueberry, blackberry, and groundcherry. But unlike raccoons, groundhogs, rabbits, and gray squirrels, they do not feed on garden crops. If you see one foraging in your garden, you should welcome it; in all probability it is rooting out hawk-moth grubs, wire worms, or beetles. Skunks are often seen in the compost heap and may appear around bird feeders on warmer evenings in late winter.

There are several species of skunks in the United States,

but the one you are most likely to see is the striped skunk. Skunks are relatively tame. Their odoriferous defense system has worked well for them in evolutionary terms, and they have little to fear. If you move slowly, you can get fairly close to a foraging skunk without problems; in fact, they are slow to use their spray and will usually warn you first by turning abruptly, raising their tails, and stamping their hind legs. If, on this signal, you retreat, they will go their way without resorting to their sole defense.

A number of people I know are so fond of skunks they have taken to feeding them. Skunks are fond of cat food, and if you happen to see one and set out a dish of food, within a week or so it will begin visiting your yard regularly. This is not necessarily a custom I would recommend, however, unless you want to start a colony. The local skunk population may begin to come *en masse,* and, fesity as they are among each other, there is bound to be a little fighting at three or four in the morning. Furthermore, at some point, one of them is bound to spray some local cat or dog, possibly your own. Worse yet, as in my case, they may begin to try to take shelter in your cellar.

Late Bloomers

Spring is the traditional season of blossoming, but there are a number of back-yard plant species that will go into flower during the shortened days of autumn. The growth and blossoming of many plants is determined by the length of daylight, and since autumn is more or less a replica of spring as far as light is concerned, you may be able to find a few flowers of spring and early summer blossoming in your yard as late as November. Typical

FALL

of these, and perhaps my favorite late autumn flower, is the hardy dandelion. In spite of the above, however, most of the flowers you will find are frost-hardy and are programmed to blossom in the cooler, drier season of autumn. Watch for them in the wild corners of your property.

Goldenrods

In northern latitudes, the first goldenrods will appear in mid-August in old fields, along roadsides, and in waste places such as parking lot edges and vacant lots. If you have left even a small section of your back yard uncut for a season, or if there is a no man's land between your property and your neighbor's, undoubtedly in this small space you will be able to find a few goldenrods blooming. They are easily recognized by the golden flaglike flower heads and their spiky, lance-shaped leaves. You may also be able to recognize them even before they flower by their pungent smell. Some species have a definite herbal scent that will be apparent when you walk through a bunch of them.

The individual goldenrods are not easy to identify. For one thing, there are approximately 125 species in the United States, and many are very similar in appearance. One of the more common ones is the Canadian goldenrod, a plant of approximately five feet with an erect, slender stem, leaves decorated with delicately branching veins, and shallow, saw-toothed margins. Check against other species of goldenrods to notice the differences.

While you are out musing over the great variety of goldenrod species, you may notice that some of them have swollen rounded spots on the upper stems. If you look carefully, you may notice that some of these swellings have a tiny hole in the middle, and if you happen to cut one open—preferably a fresh one—you will see there is a small white grub inside. This is the grub of the goldenrod gall; the larvae was hatched from an egg that was laid in the stem by the adult gall fly.

Another insect that you may see while you are out analyzing the flowers of the goldenrods is the blister beetle. There are sometimes so many of these tiny black beetles covering the golden plumes of the flower heads that it seems as if the plant had been sprinkled with black pepper or soot. The beetles are so named because in southern Europe, in the days before the advent of modern medicine, quantities of these insects were ground up to make a blistering ointment. Other species in the blister beetle family give off an ill-smelling oily fluid when they are disturbed. The beetles have an interesting way of spreading themselves about in the world. The larvae of some species will climb onto bees that are also visiting the goldenrod flower heads and will be carried off to the honey-rich hive, where they can feed at leisure. Unfortunately, the larvae are not always able to distinguish bees from flies and are occasionally carried off to certain starvation.

White Baneberry

There was a stretch of woodland behind a house I once lived in in New Jersey that had a number of wildflowers growing in it. One of the most exotic of these was a plant that we as children would never notice until late August or mid-September. At this time suddenly there would appear in the "forest," as we called it, a flower stem set with rounded white berries that looked for all the world like the eyes of a doll. Gilly Robinson, my early guide to the natural world, would always tell us

Baneberry

that Santa's elves would come to this plant in fall to collect the fruits to make dolls' eyes for Christmas.

The baneberry is indeed one of the more easily recognized fruits of late summer. The white berries are rounded, almost globular, and tipped with a prominent black mark—the iris, so to speak. The leaves look something like maple leaves; they are compound with deep lobes and sharp teeth. The conspicuous fruits of the baneberry are at once a boon and, as you might expect, a bane. They represent what the insurance people might refer to as an attractive nuisance. The interesting looking berries are often picked and sometimes eaten by small children—an unfortunate circumstance, since even a few berries can cause severe stomach cramps. The berries contain a powerful glycoside and, if consumed in quantity, can cause death. There are two species of baneberry, the red and the white. Both are toxic, and they have similar fruits, although the white is the one that produces the doll's eye.

Asters

Another common wildflower of late summer and early autumn that you might find growing along with the goldenrod is the aster. Like the goldenrods, there are many species in this genus, about 250 all told, some of which are obscure and difficult to find. Asters can be easily recognized by their daisylike flowers and the season in which they bloom. Generally this is the only flower of this type that you will see during the autumn, the other daisylike field wildflowers having long since gone to seed. Asters, by contrast, are hardy; they may bloom as late as December in the middle Atlantic states and farther south.

The earliest aster to bloom may be the rush aster, which

can be identified by its grasslike, thin leaves, and its pale violet flowers. Rough-leaved aster, with its wrinkled and obviously veined leaves, may also bloom early in the summer, along with the New York aster and a few others. Generally, as with most blooming seasons, the first plants to go into flower are located in the more northern regions and the blossoming works progressively southward as the season moves on. Asters can also be found in the West, especially on the uncultivated strips between highways and grazing or cropland, but they are far more common in the East.

Wild asters have some of the most beautiful blossoms of any wildflower. Plant breeders have refined a few species such as the New England aster for garden flowers—although the large double-flowered variety that is commonly sold is actually a different genus altogether. There is really no need, however, to go out to the nearest nursery to purchase these ubiquitous plants. They will grow readily in any uncultivated ground on your property. Or, if you insist on a more orderly, formal garden, you can dig up a few wild ones from your land and transplant them to the garden. The easiest thing to do in my view is a little of both. Allow some sections of your property to go wild, and cultivate other sections.

I take as my model for this a woman named Megan Lewis, who lived in a small cottage a mile or so through the woods on a back road in the Berkshires in western Massachusetts. Megan was about sixty-five when I met her, and for thirty-five of those years she had worked and reworked the property she and her husband had purchased in the late 1920s. She began, she told me, to make a formal garden on the property, went to the magazines and garden books of that era, setting out beds of tulips and planting a classic English dooryard garden of hollyhocks and delphiniums. But after twenty years of this, she said she grew bored of all the splendor of her creation and began taking walks in the nearby woodlands. At age fifty or so she began to notice for the first time in her life the beauty of wildflowers, and sometime in the mid 1950s she began judiciously to transplant a few of these to her land. Slowly over the next decade she allowed the hollyhocks and the delphiniums to grow wilder. She let some of her carefully cultivated flower beds go to seed, allowed patches of lawn to grow up to weeds, and began to mow narrow little trails between the uncultivated strips and the half-tended vegetable and flower gardens. Her place was not the type that would cause comment to passers-by; that is to say, there were no showy beds or smooth places to it. But once you began to explore it more intimately—ideally with Megan herself as guide–you saw the subtle designs of her land. There was not a corner of her property, not so much as a square foot, that was not thought out and worked over; and yet the land look superficially like any lush, weedy section in a forgotten corner of New England. Nevertheless, her garden would begin flowering earlier than any of her neighbors, would be in bloom late into the fall, and was a haven for birds, butterflies, bees, and small mammals.

Poison Ivy

Although it generally flowers in early summer, one of the other plants that you may notice in your yard in autumn, if you haven't found it already, is poison ivy. It turns a rich red at this time of year and may be more noticeable than it is in spring and summer. One autumn the farmer who runs the farmstand down the road from

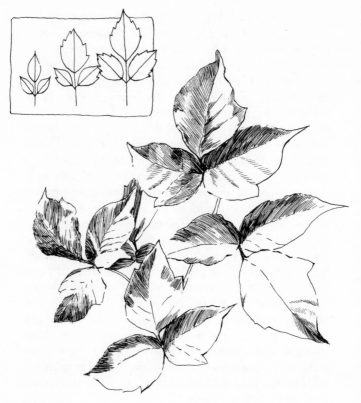

Poison Ivy

me looked out his window and saw a woman gathering
beautiful scarlet leaves from a plant that was growing
on his stone walls. In alarm, he went out and explained
that the autumn bouquet she was making up consisted
mostly of poison ivy leaves. "Don't be ridiculous," she
said. "I *know* poison ivy. It is very ugly. These leaves
are beautiful." Being a New Englander, and further-

more a man of few words, my farmer friend said "Suit yourself" and went back in the house.

Poison ivy is indeed an attractive plant. It will grow as a full shrub if given the chance; it will climb trees like a vine and will cover whole sections of forests and glades as a low, single-stemmed herbaceous plant. It is also a relatively good source of food for wild animals; some sixty-three species of birds feed on the berries or leaves. The fact that it can cause a severe allergic reaction should not prevent you from allowing at least a few of these colorful and infamous plants to grow on your property, if only as a lesson in what not to touch. Of all the plants mentioned in this guide, this is perhaps the most practical to learn to identify. Poison ivy has three leaves, but that is about all that is definitive about the plant. The leaves may or may not be shiny; the edges of the leaves may or may not be serrated, or toothed; and, as I say, the plant can grow as an herbaceous ground cover, a shrub, or a vine. Nevertheless, once you learn to recognize the basic shape, you will notice that poison ivy is in some regions one of the most common plants in the woods, and, true to form, it grows in deep, shaded woods as well as open fields and waste places.

Mushrooms

Any mushrooms that you find in your backyard generally can be divided into two types, those with gills or radiating paper-thin membranes underneath their caps and those with pores, spongelike bottoms, pocked with pinholes. Once you learn these basic differences, you can begin to fine-tune your mushroom identification skills. And if you confine yourself to the mushrooms that grow in your back yard, and you use a good field guide, you will find that within a single season you will know all the mushrooms that grow on your property. They come up year after year, pretty much in the same general area, so once you know where to expect the individual species, you will probably have few surprises.

Puffballs

Some of the most common back-yard fungi are edible. One of these, the puffball, comes up after rains in late summer and early fall and has none of the characteristics of the mushrooms described above. When it is small, it looks like a smooth golf ball lost in the grass. Given time—sometimes overnight if the conditions are right— it will grow to the size of a baseball. And given more time, no more than a day or two, it will grow to the size of a softball. Some may continue on to basketball size, but these are rarer. Puffballs are edible. If you cut them in half and the flesh is white and firm, they are still "ripe." Yellow or soft places are an indication that the mushroom is aging and will not taste good, although it is not necessarily poisonous at this stage.

Puffballs are sometimes confused with another mushroom, known as the deadly amanita, or the destroying angel, which may also grow in back yards that are or were wooded. When amanitas are young they look very much like tiny puffballs. They are associated with trees, but if you live on land that has been cleared and the stumps were left in the ground, they may grow on your property. Generally the most toxic amanitas can be recognized by the ring around the stem, the cuplike ball that the stem grows out of and the pure white cap and white gills. The entire embryonic mushroom is contained in the cup before it opens. If you happen to have puffballs in your yard and you decide to try a few, check a mushroom guide book to make sure you have the right species, and then be sure to cut each puffball down the middle and inspect the inside. If it is an amanita, you will see the embryonic stem and cap curled up inside the cup.

Puffballs will shrivel after a few days, and a tiny hole will appear in the top of the ball. If, at this stage, you tap the ball lightly, a tiny puff of brown powder will appear—not unlike a miniature volcano plume. This brown powder is made up of the spores of the puffball. The fungi will continue puffing out until the spores of the ball are empty. Considering the fact that from any one of the specks of dust theoretically a new puffball could be produced, it seems incredible that the world is not buried in these common fungi. Yet the dynamics of growth and development are such that the exact conditions of moisture, soil chemistry, and nutrient loading are necessary for the mushroom to take hold.

Whenever I discover puffballs, I always allow a few to go wild. In fact, I send out my children to tap on them in order to help spread the spores, one of the few chores they take on willingly.

Boletes

If you have a wooded yard, after a rain in mid-summer and again in the fall you might be able to find a few species of boletes on your land. These fungi belong to the group that contain pores beneath their caps and are fairly easy to recognize. They generally have a rounded cap like a roll or a bun; the stems are swollen or fattened; and, of course, unlike the gilled mushrooms, the underside of the caps are dotted with hundreds of tiny holes.

The bolete group contains some of the species most

King Bolete

sought after by mushroom fanciers. In some places in Europe there is fierce competition over picking sites; and special trains are run in Eastern Europe to carry urban mushroom eaters out into the countryside for gathering forays. One of the prizes sought by these erstwhile gourmets—and by their American counterparts—is the king bolete, a humble mushroom with a muffinlike cap and a stem that tapers outward at the base. The stem is adorned with a fine white mesh. Be sure to watch for it if you have pine trees on your property.

A few boletes are poisonous, and more than a few, although not toxic, have a bitter taste and are considered inedible, but an equal number are considered to be among the finest in the wide array of edible mushrooms found throughout the United States and Canada. There is a test you can use to determine if the bolete you have found is edible, although as with all mushrooms and in fact any edible plant, you should check your reference books carefully before eating. For one thing, boletes always grow on the ground. If you find a mushroom that looks like a bolete growing on wood, it is something else. Furthermore, if you draw your fingernail across a bolete or break it open and notice that it develops a bluish stain, discard it. Generally it appears that mushrooms with this tendency are somewhat toxic. Finally, if the bolete has red pores underneath the cap, don't eat it. Although the red-pored boletes are not necessarily deadly and a few are even edible, some of them can make you decidedly ill.

Fairy Rings

Some summer morning you may notice a group of small, brownish mushrooms with slender stalks growing in a circular or semicircular pattern on your lawn. If you happen to find some of these altogether common mushrooms, you should count yourself lucky—or unlucky, depending upon how you feel about fairies. According to folklore, the night before, while you were asleep, forces were at work in your back yard. The slender brown mushrooms are said to appear only in the path fairies use during their circular night dances; hence the common name for this mushroom. The fairy ring is about three to four inches high and has a wooly stalk and light brown to white gills. It is edible and considered choice eating, but since there are a number of small, lawn-growing species that are inedible, it is probably best left alone, unless you can get positive identification.

There is another theory to account for the circular growth pattern of the fairy ring and other species of mushrooms. Fungi such as the fairy ring grow from an underground netlike body known as the mycelium, which is the permanent part of the plant. The mushrooms you see growing after rains are merely the fruiting bodies of the mycelium and are somewhat analogous to flowers. Since the mycelium seeks the most nutrient rich soil medium, in lawns, where the food supply is often uniformly spread, the mycelium grows ever outward in a circular pattern as the soil in the center of the ring becomes depleted.

Meadow Mushrooms

One of the other mushrooms that you might find in your yard if you are lucky is a fungi with an off-white cap that looks very much like a larger version of the mushroom you buy in the grocery store. The similarity is logical, since this is the species of mushroom from which the commercial variety was developed. The meadow mushroom has a whitish cap and pink gills when it is younger, which, as the mushroom ages, turn a rich brown color. Although the store-bought mushroom is now recognized as a different species, the two are so similar that it is fairly safe to say that if you find a mushroom in your yard that looks like the mushrooms in your refrigerator, it is probably the meadow mushroom and probably safe to eat. As always, though, it is best to get positive identification before you try it. Make sure that the meadow mushrooms on your property do not have the veil or ring around the stem—one of the defining characteristics of mushrooms in the genus amanita.

Meadow mushrooms use to come up in one of my yards. They would appear, it seemed to me, at the oddest times, with seemingly little respect for good mushroom behavior. Then one year, for no apparent reason, they failed to come up at all and, to my knowledge, ceased to exist in that area altogether. They also had the habit of turning brown quickly, so that if I didn't get to them on the first or second day, they would be squishy or dried out or riddled with insects. Nevertheless, the ones I managed to capture were among the most delectable mushrooms I have eaten. They had a stronger, fuller mushroom taste than any of the store-bought varieties, a sort of bounty-of-the-earth flavor that reeked of wholeness and the good life. I enjoyed them for the three or four years that I inhabited that land and since then have never had the good fortune to have a yard in which they came up.

Ferns

There was a time when ferns were more appreciated as garden plants then they are in our time. No shady nook of the nineteenth-century town garden was complete without a few stands of wood ferns or more exotic species, such as the ostrich fern. Peruse any collection of photographs of home gardens from the turn of the century and you will likely see them there, as lacy and lush then as they are now—you can almost smell the rank, moist fern scent even through the decades. Ferns seem to have gone out of style somewhat as garden plants, but the wild ones will move in to any unmanaged shady part of your property if given half a chance. And if they don't move in, you can always get some at your local nursery. They are among the most delicately beautiful of all nonflowering plants.

Wood Ferns

Ferns have a complex life cycle involving, in place of flowers and the production of pollen, the release of spores into the air. Wherever the spores land, if the conditions are right, a tiny one-celled body known as the prothallus will begin growing, and from this the mature fern plant will develop. On many species of ferns the spore-bearing cases look like tiny dots, and from the position of these dots, and from the shape and cut of the leaves of the fern, you can identify the species. In the common, marginal wood fern these spore cases are found along the edges of the leaflets of the ferns and develop sometime in late July or August.

Marginal wood fern is also known as evergreen wood fern; along with Christmas fern, which has tiny boot-shaped leathery leaflets, it is one of the few ferns that stays green throughout the year. Look for stands of evergreen wood fern in rocky wooded sections of your yard, if you happen to have such a habitat. In New England it can commonly be found beside the old stone walls that criss-cross the landscape; look there if you happen to have an old wall on your property. Christmas fern may also grow beside old walls, but more commonly it is found near large rocks or boulders.

Sensitive Fern

You may not at first recognize this one as a fern. Sensitive fern, unlike its ferny brothers and sisters, has broad, flattened leaves, very much like a flowering plant. It grows commonly in wet areas but will also do well on

Sensitive Fern

any low ground and seems to grow as easily in sun as it does in shade. The leaves of this fern are veined, also like a flowering plant, and if you find one sensitive fern, you are likely to find many; they seem to prefer growing in groups. Someday in late September or October you will notice that, quite abruptly, all the sensitive ferns in your yard have disappeared. This species is very sensitive to frost; hence its name.

After the leaves die back, the fern will leave behind an upright brownish stalk with little branches at the top that are covered with what appear to be tiny beebees. This is the spore-bearing body of the fern, corresponding to the fruit dots, or sori, which appear on the margins of the leaflet of the wood fern. You may find other ferns in your yard that have leafless spore-bearing stalks. Growing among the leaves of the cinnamon fern, for example, you may see a stiff, clublike stalk that is bright green when young but turns to a rich cinnamon color as it ages. Ostrich fern, once commonly sold as an ornamental fern, also has a spore-bearing stalk, shaped a little like a lyre.

Early in the spring before the fern fronds uncoil themselves, they are tightly rolled in a small circular stalk known commonly as the fiddlehead. The fiddleheads of some species of ferns are edible; in fact, they are delicious, vying, in the opinion of some, with the early shoots of asparagus. The only problem is that some fiddleheads are too bitter to eat, so you have to locate the good stands of the edible species during the summer and then come back during the right week in spring to catch the ferns in the fiddlehead stage. The most widely consumed fiddlehead is the bracken, although there was a nasty and unsubstantiated rumor around for a while suggesting that this fern causes cancer. Ostrich fern fiddleheads also make good eating. In the past, wild food foragers would consume the fiddleheads of the cinnamon fern, although these have a decidedly acrid taste. While ostrich and cinnamon fern may be found in your yard, bracken seems to prefer old pastures and waste places. It is actually one of the more common ferns in many areas, but the lush, limey verdure of the backyard seems to repel it; you may have to go to your nearest old field or woodlot if you are intent on gathering these fiddleheads.

Daddy Longlegs

Mid-autumn is the time of year when you are most likely to encounter the spiderlike arachnid known as the harvestman, or daddy longlegs. The young, which hatch in spring, have matured by fall and can often be seen in sections of your yard that you have allowed to go wild, or at those important lanes of untended land between or along property lines. Watch for them also in woodpiles and on old logs or along walls.

Daddy longlegs are so familiar as to hardly need description. They have tiny, brown bodies and look a little like a Rice Crispie set atop absurdly long legs. The circular pattern of the harvestman's legs probably gives rise to one of those wise little tidbits of folklore that is associated with this arachnid. Legend holds that the daddy longlegs will always point to cows. Since the legs point in all directions, and since the daddy longlegs are commonly found in pastures and meadows, they in fact *do* point to cows—as well as to sheep, horses, goats, people, houses, and anything else in the general vicinity. This is undoubtedly one of those legends that was invented specifically to entertain children; no one over ten would fall for the trick.

Harvestmen feed on small insects and other arthropods and may also act as scavengers, feeding on dead or decaying matter. They generally feed at night, although they are commonly seen during the day. They do not bite, but some species will give off an unpleasant odor if handled or disturbed, and most of them will jettison a leg or two if you grab it. The best way to catch them, or to look at them more closely, is simply to allow them to walk over your hand. That way there will be no apparent disturbance and no lost legs.

LATE

FALL

THERE IS FOR ME, for some reason, great depth of meaning in the spare, barren landscape of late fall. There is something about the slanting afternoon shadows, the sere browns and grays of the fields, and the rich, umber-colored woodlands that brings up memories. It is a phenomenon that I have been told others experience. The general ambience and sense of nostalgia may come from the fact that at this time of year it becomes all too clear that the languorous days of summer, Indian summer, and autumn are indeed at an end and the hardships of winter are about to set in.

And yet November and early December have a beauty of their own. If you stay out-of-doors for more than a half-hour or so, the subtler details of this darker season come into clear focus. This is a time of small specialties, the last blooming of the dandelion or asters or chrysanthemums, the last plaintive call of the field crickets, and the first thin whistle and chirps of the incoming winter migrants such as juncos and winter finches. The last leaves have been raked from the yard, and if you have a fireplace or a woodstove, the last stacks of firewood have been piled and repiled in preparation for the onset of the cold season. This is the time of year to look for all the tings that the foliage of summer has hidden away, the birds' nests, the leafy balls of squirrels' nests in the crotches of trees, the dead hanging limbs, and less natural things—toys lost in the shrubbery or tools left behind.

I have made a point over the past few years of keeping a record of when things end. Many people keep a record of when things begin, but to my knowledge, natural history diaries do not specialize in endings. The records make interesting reading. You will probably notice, if you keep one, that things end on schedule, just as they more or less begin on schedule during the springtime. For example, in my area, the last meadow crickets can generally be heard around December 7; the snowy tree crickets, by contrast, stop calling around the middle of October; the last dandelions bloom around November 12, and the milkweeds in the field across from my house burst their pods just before Thanksgiving.

It is true that with the onset of winter—the closing down of the natural world and of the garden—there seems

Field Cricket

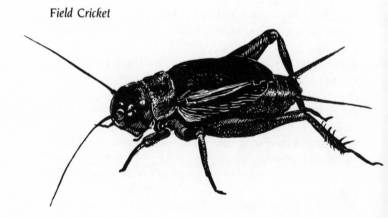

to be less to do out-of-doors. But to my way of think-ing, that is all the more reason to find something to do out in the yard. A natural history diary helps. But I have also gotten in the habit (have always been in the habit, actually) of taking coffee or lunch outdoors at this time of year—weather permitting, of course. I have also got-ten into the habit of periodically stepping outdoors at night to see what is happening, and as a result have seen or heard a lot of little changes taking place that I might have missed otherwise—the clamoring call of geese passing in the night or the high chirp of migratory songbirds. Eating outdoors, or simply sitting in the yard until the chill of winter either drives you inside or forces you into some kind of activity, will help you to stay in touch with this elusive, transitory season.

Club Mosses

If you live in one of those neighborhoods where devel-opers stripped off all the native vegetation and then replanted houses, you are not likely to find club moss on your property. On the other hand, if the buildres fit the houses between the trees, so to speak, and left as much native vegetation as possible, you may find a few patches of these beautiful plants growing in the shady parts of your land.

The club mosses are a plant for all seasons. They stay green throughout the year; large patches of this moss may provide the only extensive areas of green in the fall and winter woods, and they put up the club moss ver-sion of a flower in the spring and summer. In general, club mosses look like tiny pine trees, some like white pines, some like miniature spruces. Viewed close up, and especially through a hand lens or the lens of a camera, they look like whole forests. And if you get even closer and sniff deeply, you will notice that they invariably give off the rich scent of the essential earth, a dank musk that permeates the autumnal forests after a rain.

During the latter part of the last century and the early part of the twentieth century people reuglarly used to leave the cities around Christmastime to collect plants in the club moss family to make Christmas wreaths. What was once a hobby became something of a small industry involving professional collectors, and in time, as is often the case in such situations, the plants began to disappear. Fortunately, laws protecting these humble mosses were passed in various states, and they are now generally protected, so look and enjoy, but do not pick.

There was another use for these plants during the nineteenth century. Club mosses are primitive plants; their ancestors were once a part of the great fern forests that covered the earth during the Paleozoic era some three hundred million years ago. They predate flowering plants, reproducing themselves by means of spores, a yellow pollenlike dust that you can see, and even collect if you care to, by touching the spore-bearing body of these evergreens. The spores are highly volatile, and during the nineteenth century the dust was collected and used on stage as flash powder to introduce such entertaining figures as the devil. The powder was also used in the flash trays of early cameras and was sometimes used for medicinal purposes as a soothing powder.

There are about eleven species in the continental United States. Some are relatively rare or at least highly localized, so this is an easy plant group to get to know. Once you begin to learn the subtle differences among the species, they are easy to separate; and you can often find three or four different members of this group in a small area. They have, to my mind, wonderfully descriptive common names—wolf's-claw club moss, for example, Robin Hood's hatband, forks and knives, or tree-branched club moss. One of the most common is the shining club moss, which can be recognized by its upright branches covered with bright shiny needles. Wolf's-claw club moss, another relatively common species in some areas, as opposed to the shining club, has many branches, which look very much like antlers; in fact, another common name for the plant is staghorn club moss. Wolf's-claw is one of the species of club moss that was gathered for Christmas decorations, so it is not as common as it once was in those few remaining patches of woodlands near cities—you probably won't find it if you live in an older suburb. Tree club moss looks like its name—a young pine tree about six inches in height, its trunk and limbs covered with bristly needles. Ground cedar, or princess pine, one of the most beautiful of the club mosses, also looks very like a tree, a cedar in this case. It is a symmetrical plant with tiny, fanlike spreading branches that are coated with tightly clustered lance-shaped needles. Running ground pine is fairly similar in appearance but less regular in its branching habit.

Hair-cap Moss

A closely related but somewhat more pedestrian group of mosses are the hair-cap mosses. These sometimes grow in large patches of poor soil, either wet or dry and, like the club mosses, create the impression of extensive miniature forests when viewed close up. They also have the rich earth smell of the club mosses and, furthermore, make a soft bed to lie on during late summer afternoons. If you have a shady lawn under older trees, you may have sections of this moss growing side by side with lawn grass. Wild grasses and small weeds tend to invade

Hair-cap Moss

patches of the hair-cap moss, and to my mind, it is such a delicate and beautiful plant that it is worth weeding your wild patch now and then to keep the mat of moss in place.

There are three common species of hair-cap mosses. The so-called common hair-cap moss usually grows in large stands covering areas that may be yards across. Juniper hair-cap moss has a sharp-tipped leaf or needle that looks very much like the leaves of a cedar or juniper. It, too, is fairly common, although it tends to grow in dry soil, whereas the common hair-cap seems to prefer slightly damp areas and does well in open sun. The hair-cap moss known as Slender Catherinea is more common in the northeastern states and seems to prefer half-shaded drier soil.

Hair-cap mosses are named for the slender fruiting body that these plants put up each year. The male and female organs are carried on separate plants. The female part is an elongated spike that looks a little like a folded umbrella in the common hair-cap moss. The male appendage looks like a tiny cylinder on the end of a stalk. The tube, or cylinder, is capped with a pyramid-shaped "hat." If you touch this cap when it is ripe, it will literally flip its lid, sending off a little plume of yellow dust— the spores of the hair-cap moss.

Pincushion Moss

Growing near the common hair-cap mosses in your yard you may be able to find a delicate, rounded clump of green moss that looks like a pincushion. This aptly named moss grows in shade, sometimes on trees or rotting logs. It may grow to five or six inches across and in wet weather is perhaps one of the more beautiful common mosses. It has a rich, velvety green color and, like many of these humble plants, has a wonderful smell. Back in the days of smaller pleasures when boys and girls used to forage through the woods collecting plants for terrariums, this was one of the more sought-after mosses. It still does well in captivity, although in my opinion, like most plants and animals it looks better in the wild.

Pincushion moss grows throughout the United States and usually puts up its tiny stalked spore case from autumn through to spring; look for it whenever there is no snow cover. During dry periods it more or less shrivels into a sad, borwnish version of its lush, green, autumnal self. It becomes dry and brittle and will crumble if you pick it up and crush it.

Common Fern Moss

If you see a closely branched fernlike plant growing or creeping across a moist rock or an old stump or log on your property, you are probably looking at one of the six species of fern moss that can be found from Labrador to British Columbia and south to the Gulf of Mexico. This plant, like the pincushion moss, is one of those under-appreciated plants that has a definitive and even exquisite beauty to it when viewed close up. Its light green stem, crowded with tightly bunched featherlike leaves, branches again and again as the plant sprawls over whatever object it happens to be growing on. Given the proper habitat—plenty of moisture and shade, that is— the plant may cover an area of several feet, although the ones I have seen have never covered more than six or seven square inches of a rock or log.

Lichens

One of the delights involved in the exploration of the mosses in your back yard is the other discoveries you are likely to make. Shrinking your focus so that you

begin to notice the smaller things can open an entire
wilderness in the space of a few square yards. One of
the most colorful of the plants in this wilderness is the
British soldier lichen, a gray-green collection of tiny
upright stems capped with bright red. Except for their
color, the lichens look like a jumble of tiny matchsticks
stuck in the ground or on a decaying log. More often
than not, they grow with the mosses mentioned above.
There is a closely related lichen, the Pixie Cup, which
has instead of a bright red cap a funnel-like top. Pixie
cups survive in drier conditions than the British soldier
lichen and may even grow on tree turnks and dead wood
that has dried in the sun. Both lichens are common and
widespread, although the British soldier does not regularly grow west of the Rockies.

Reindeer Moss

This lichen may also be found in the same general area
as the mosses and British soldiers. It, too, often forms
large patches some yards or more across. In the tundra,
where it is extremely common and is one of the pre-
ferred foods of the reindeer and caribou, it grows exten-
sively. The fact that this plant is eaten by reindeer suggests
some kind of uncanny order to the universe. If you look
carefully at the plant, you will see that the patch consists
of thousands of tiny, gray, branchlike stems that look
very much like the antlers of a reindeer. As with all
lichens, reindeer moss is a combination of two plants,
an alga and a fungus. The green alga, with its chloro-
phyll, helps gather nutrients for the plant through
photosynthesis; the fungus helps break down organic
and inorganic material on which the plant grows. Both
lichens and mosses are primary soil builders. They break
down inorganic material, die and decay, and in the process build up a layer of soil. Lichens, for example, will

grow on a base of granite. In time they will build up enough of a soil base—thin though it may be—for mosses to take hold. The mosses in turn will die back, thereby creating enough soils for other species of mosses, liverworts, and ferns, which in turn will decay to create a suitable soil medium for higher plants, such as wildflowers, shrubs, and tree seedlings. For these reasons it is best to leave these small pioneers in place. Soil is a precious commodity.

Sphagnum Moss

There is one other moss that you may find on your property. Sphagnum moss generally grows in bogs and in wet areas, so if you have it on your land, the chances are your house was constructed on fill over a fresh-water wetland—not an uncommon situation in some parts of the country. If you have a cellar that is often flooded in spring, or if you have sections of your yard that are exceedingly damp, you might look for this interesting and valuable moss.

Sphagnum is one of those plants that has made it into the history books. For one thing, it is the pioneer plant of wetlands, the very creator, in fact, of the wetlands known as bogs. Sphagnum will grow in still waters that are slightly acidic, and since these conditions occurred over most of the northern hemisphere in the centuries after the glaciers retreated some 15,000 years ago, it managed to spread itself throughout most of the northern half of the American and European continents. It is a great land builder; as it dies back, it sinks to the bottom in progressive layers so that in time—that is, after a few hundred years or more—it will ground out and the open waters will turn into a mucky, soggy expanse known technically as a bog. The resulting soil is known as peat, itself a valuable commodity. In northern Europe and the British Isles, peat is mined and dried and used for fuel, and in this country and Europe, it is dug, packaged, and sold to gardeners to improve the texture of soil. Sphagnum moss is extremely absorbent. If you find it on your land, grab a handful and squeeze it and you will see that a great fall of water will pour out, more water than you would believe could possibly be contained in so small a bundle of plant material. Because of this absorbency, in the early part of this century it was dried and used for bandages or gauze.

Sphagnum is easy enough to recognize, since it grows only in wet areas. It is almost always soggy or at least damp, and on close inspection the individual plant stems look a little like thoroughly soaked spruce trees.

Bird Nests

Quite abruptly some morning in late fall, generally after a night of high winds or rain, you will awaken to find that all the leaves have disappeared from the trees. Suddenly the stark new world of brambles and bare branches will become strikingly evident, and for the first time you will be able to see clearly the nesting spots of all the summer birds. It is a somewhat sad event in its own way. The bright songsters are gone, the nestlings are fledged and have flown south, and all that is left to remember them by are a few brown clumps of dried grasses and twigs.

I am always taken aback by the first stripping of the leaves in November. I keep a careful check on the birds that nest on my land, and yet I am always surprised by the number that I have missed. Here, not ten yards from the house, I will find the nest of some obscure sparrow or finch woven into the tangled branches of the hedge, or high in the oaks I will see the blot of twigs marking the site of some unidentifiable tree dweller.

One important note on birds' nests: Except for a few species, like ospreys and eagles, birds build a new nest every year, so theoretically, if you were so inclined, you could collect the nest and take it indoors. But in the interest of protecting nests that are still occupied, the federal government has passed a law that forbids the possession of nests. The law may be a hangover from the days when nest and egg collecting were in full vogue; nevertheless, it does serve its purpose, so look, but don't take. Besides, the white-footed mouse has a habit of taking up residence in abandoned bird nests (see page 164).

Crested Flycatcher

Some birds have a way of weaving into their nests some characteristic plant material, such as vine bark, string, or horsehair. Typical of these is the great crested flycatcher. For whatever reason, this bird has been programmed by evolution to include a shed snakeskin in its nest. If it cannot find a skin, it will resort to modern technological advances and substitutte cellophane or a strip of polyethylene sheeting. The nest is generally constructed in a natural cavity, such as a woodpecker hole or sometimes even a birdhouse. Along with the obligatory snakeskin, the crested flycatcher uses twigs, leaves, and bark fibers to complete the construction, altogether a rather bulky and disorganized mass of material. Look for the nest in dead trees about ten to twelve feet above the ground.

Mockingbird

Watch for the mockingbird's nest in small trees or shrubs or, more commonly, in a tangle of vines or a thicket.

The nest is constructed from twigs, stiff grasses, and weed stems and may have bits of rags or string woven into it.

Robin

Robins sometimes nest on the ledge of a building or a post, but more often the nest can be found in the crotch of a tree or on the outer branches. The nest consists of a bulky, untidy arrangement of grasses and weeds bound together, on occasion, with bits of string. The inside of the nest is lined with a cup of mud mixed with fine grasses, a perfectly shaped structure that constrasts dramatically with the disorganized exterior.

Wood Thrush

Wood thrushes, which are related to robins, also line their nests with mud, as do most thrushes. Wood thrush nests tend to have a middle layer of mud in the walls, mixed with dead leaves and a cup that is lined with rootlets or leaves. The outside of the nest is made from weed stems and grasses. The nest is usually found in the fork of a sapling or small tree, about ten feet above the ground.

Yellow-throat Warbler

Yellow-throats generally nest near water—a swamp, for example, or a small stream or creek; but I regularly find a yellow-throat nest in a thicket beside a road in front of my house. The nest is small and usually no more than three feet off the ground. It is cup-shaped and is constructed from weed stems and leaves, as well as ferns, bark strips, and vine tendrils. Occasionally the yellow-throat will build a wall or hood of loose material up over the rim of the nest.

LATE FALL

Northern Oriole

Of all the birds' nests, the northern oriole's is perhaps the easiest to recognize. If you haven't spotted it during nesting season, and you have one near your property, you will undoubtedly see it after the leaves fall from the trees. The nest is often placed over a road or driveway at the tip of a branch about twenty to thirty feet above the ground. It is an unmistakable pouchlike arrangement constructed from vines, bark, hair, string, plant fibers, and any other available stringy material. The inside of the pouch is lined with hair, wool, fine grasses, and plant down. As the winter progresses, these gray, drooping pouches are invariably torn apart by high winds so that by the end of the season they end up looking like nothing more than a few mere shreds of forlorn litter dangling from the branches.

Catbird

Catbirds, like the yellowthroats, may also nest near water, but in my experience they also nest in the dense shrubbery around suburban houses. The nest is usually about six to ten feet above the ground and is constructed from sticks, leaves, and weeds and lined with rootlets and bark shreds. The lining may also contain pine needles or hair and even bits of cotton. This is another one of those nests that you are likely to discover during the nesting season. Catbirds are extremely vocal around their nest, whining and meowing the summer long; they are also relatively tame. If you remember regularly hearing or seeing a catbird in your yard during the previous summer, check your bushes after the leaves are off the trees; you will probably find a nest.

Wren

Another local nester who will usually make its presence
known during the nesting season is the wren. The house
wren nests in a cavity or, more often than not—unfortunately—in bluebird or tree swallow nest boxes. But
other wrens, the Carolina and the winter wren, for
example, make a domed nest constructed from weed
stems and bark strips. You may find that you have more
wren nests than wrens, since the male is polygamous
and tends to build a number of nests in its territory,
some of which may never be occupied by a female.

House Wren

Vireo

Watch for vireo nests at the end of branches in small trees or shrubs around your house. This is one of those nests that may surprise you. Vireos are not easy to spot, and unlike the catbird or the wren are not particularly active around the yard or their nests; so unless you are alert during the nesting season, you may have no indication that one raised its young in your territory. The nests are usually suspended from twig forks, are attached at the rim, and may be lined with fine plant fibers, spider webs, and hair. Some vireos nest quite high up, so unless the winds dislodge one, you are not likely to get a close look. But, although they feed high in the branches, the red-eyed and the solitary vireo may place their nests no more than six feet above the ground. A solitary vireo nested several years in succession in the lower branches of a hickory tree not far from a relatively busy road near a house where I once lived. Even though I knew there were solitary vireos about during the summer, I was never able to find the nests until November.

Holes in Trees

There are a number of species of birds around suburban homes that make their nests in tree trunks. Woodpeckers, in particular, are hole nesters; but there are other species, such as the chickadee and the nuthatch, that will also either drill or find existing holes for their nests. Other than cutting out the nest hole area with a chain saw, the only way to identify which hole belongs to which species of bird is through observation of the bird itself or the size of the hole. For example, the hairy woodpecker, which is a bird about the size of a robin, usually makes a hole about two to two and a half inches high and an inch and a half or so across. Its smaller relative, the downy woodpecker, makes a hole that is about an inch and a half in diameter. Flickers have holes that are about two to four inches in diameter, and the common red-headed woodpecker makes a hole slightly under two inches. You can also guess at the identity of the hole maker by the state of the tree. Downy woodpeckers and red-headeds prefer dead trees, whereas the hairy makes its hole generally in a living tree.

A freshly excavated hole usually indicates a woodpecker nest cavity. If the hole looks older or appears to have healed some of its wounds, in all probability another species is using the nest. Flycatchers often nest in the holes of large woodpeckers, whereas smaller birds like the chickadee and the nuthatch will nest in the holes of the downy woodpecker.

Inside the hole, the woodpecker will chisel out a cavity and lay the eggs at the base, sometimes on the bare wood. Gray squirrels may beat the flycatchers to the old nest holes of larger woodpeckers, enlarge the entrance by gnawing away at the edges, and raise a winter brood in the hollow. Tree holes are something of a premium in the suburban animal world—they offer excellent shelter from the weather and from predators, for one thing; and so it is possible that an older woodpecker hole, enlarged by squirrels, will also shelter a possum or even a raccoon. It makes no difference to the birds. The woodpeckers make a new hole each year.

Hornet's Nests

Another nest that may appear in the trees or shrubbery around your house after the leaves are gone is the globular gray nest of the bald-faced hornet. You may have noticed the nest earlier in the year, during the summertime. You may even have attempted to eradicate it, an

Bald-faced Hornet's Nest

event that more often than not ends in disaster. If you do find a hornet's nest in the summer, as long as it is not located in a particularly busy part of your yard it is probably best left alone. Bald-faced hornets, or white-faced, as they are sometimes called, look ferocious, have a bad reputation, and can inflict a genuinely painful sting, but in general they are relatively docile creatures that take other pest species such as mosquitoes and flies. I had no fewer than two nests in my yard one year and used to entertain myself by watching the hornets snatch flies above my head as I lay in a hammock in the back yard.

On the other hand, any attempt to break up the nest will inevitably cause them to marshall their forces, and they will stream out in an angry horde to search out and sting the nest destroyer. In any case, winter will do the work for you if you are patient enough. As the autumn progresses, the queens in the hive begin to disperse. They will seek out individual hibernating spots in old logs and similar spots and spend the winter in dormancy. The other members of the hive will continue to forage for a while, but as the cold weather sets in, they will gradually die off. This means that any hive you find in your yard after the heavy frosts will probably be empty. You can safely take it down or even bring it into your house. The queens will construct a new nest in the following spring.

If you strip off the outer layers, you will be able to see what an elaborate construction you have lived side by side with all summer. The papery outer walls are laid on, layer after layer, around a central cylinder of combs, each containing tiny brood chambers where the larvae were raised. There may be as many as 2,000 cells in a large nest, some big, some smaller. Workers were produced in the smaller cells, males in the larger. The nest itself may be plastered or layered around the fork of a branch or around several small branches—a thoroughly secure construction. The winter wind may tear apart the outer layers as the season progresses, but the first foundations of the nest will probably remain wrapped around the twigs until the following season.

Hawks, Squirrels, and Crows

You may also notice after the leaves are off the trees a bulky construction in the crotch of some high tree, which the uninitiated invariably refer to as a hawk's nest. The nest may indeed be that of a hawk, but it might also be a squirrel's nest, the nest of a crow, or even the nest of an owl. The gray squirrel raises its young in two different nests during the year. In the colder months, it lives in holes in trees, usually, as pointed out earlier, in an old woodpecker hole chiseled out to make room for the adult squirrel. In the warmer seasons, however, squirrels build bulky leaf nests high in the trees, generally in the crotch of the main trunk. Like many birds' nests, these summer homes are generally obscured from view during the growing season, but once the leaves are gone, you can spot them easily.

If you look carefully, you may note that some of the bulky masses consist primarily of sticks assembled in a seemingly random jumble. In this case, given the location—i.e., suburbia—the nest is probably that of a crow. But the nest of several species of hawks, such as the red-tailed hawk, the broad-winged hawk, and the Swainson's hawk, also build nests of sticks. Furthermore, barred owls and great-horned owls, both of which can often be found in developed areas, sometimes make nests on top of old crow or hawk nests. Since all of these nests are located high in trees, unless you scale the tree and analyze the linings of the nests and other signs (such as the presence of owl pellets), it may be hard to determine which is which. Red-tailed hawks and Swainson's hawks often build large bulky nests, and crows often nest in pine trees, whereas the broad-winged hawk rarely does; but until you become familiar with the nest sizes, you might not be able to tell the difference.

The Ecology of the Bird Feeder

It is, of course, an instructive thing to keep a bird feeder outside your window, to learn the various species that visit the feeder and enjoy the color, the calls, and the constant flow of activity. While you are watching the birds beyond your windows, you might take note of the ecological dynamics that are at work. The same biological rules that apply in the wildest, most remote wilderness areas are affecting the birds that come to your kitchen window each morning. You may notice, even if you were unaware of feeding customs, that certain species of birds always feed on the ground, whereas others eat only at the feeder tray. You might also notice that these two groups are colored differently. The ground feeders, especially the sparrows, are generally striped and are often light-colored underneath. The stripes and the light underbelly help to break up the overall silhouette of the bird, making it more difficult to spot. The birds that feed higher up, while they may be patterned, do not seem to need the camouflage that the ground feeders require. Since these birds spend most of their time in trees, they are somewhat less vulnerable to ground-dwelling predators such as weasels and cats.

If you study your loyal feeder population carefully,

Tree Sparrow

among birds of the same species and to some extent among the different species, you may see that there is a hierarchy. The classic pecking order, so well recognized among chickens, also is at work in the wild. If you study the details carefully, you will notice that each individual bird has some identifying characteristic; and if you keep a record of the comings and goings at your feeder, you will see that certain individuals feed upon arrival, while the others wait their turn in the nearby shrubs. If there is an intrusion, if one attempts to break the rules, there will be a certain amount of squabbling among these simple, apparently kind-hearted denizens. You will also be able to see, once you are alerted to the phenomenon, that certain species are dominant at the feeder. A flock of jays can disperse a group of chickadees, for example, and the squadrons of evening grosbeaks that descend on feeders periodically will drive away even the most determined bluejays.

Finally, although it is not common, someday you may see all the birds at your feeder—the bluejays, the ground feeders, and even the grosbeaks disperse in a flash. Following this, you will see a blue-gray streak whip past your window and grasp some unfortunate junco in its talons before returning to the nearby tree or shrub. Cooper's hawks and sharp-shinned hawks, both of which commonly feed on woodland birds, are ever alert to congregations of wild birds; and if you are fortunate enough to have any of these predators in your neighborhood, periodically at some time in the winter one will probably show up.

You might as well enjoy the display, gruesome as it may seem. There is nothing you can do—short of halting your bird-feeding activities altogether, in which case the hawks will continue their bird killing in the nearby woods. Life goes on at the feeder, and if you are going to keep one, you might as well appreciate the dynamics of the food chain.

Mammals at the Bird Feeder

Birds are not the only animals that will visit your bird feeder. You may notice, if you look carefully in the snow, the long grasses beneath the feeder, or the loose soil, the criss-crossing tunnels of the meadow voles (see page 262). It is unlikely that you will see the voles themsleves; they are relatively secretive, although extremely common. They are voracious seed eaters, so it is only natural that they would, in time, find the ample supply of spilled seed beneath the feeder. And once they have discovered the larder, it is probable that they will remain for the season, taking advantage of the easy fare.

If you are one of those people who feeds fruit or suet to the birds in winter, you may also spot a skunk or two beneath the feeder early in the evening or shortly after dark. Skunks are decided opportunists and will not overlook the spilled seeds, the discarded fruit, or the suet if they can get at it.

The deer mouse may also forage for seeds near the feeder; and since these are tree-climbing mice, they may also manage to get inside the feeder itself. These mice feed at night, as you may have noticed if you happen to have any in your house, so you probably won't see them. On the other hand, if you want to get a good view of the mammal activity that takes place at your feeder on a winter night, you might set up an outdoor spotlight aimed at the general area. On of the things you might see in your feeder if you are lucky is a flying squirrel. Unlike their cousins, the gray, the fox squirrels, and the red squirrels, they are nocturnal. With a light, you may be able to see them and observe splendid, floating leaps.

You will also see, undoubtedly, a number of gray squirrels, or if you live anywhere in the North, spruce squirrels and red squirrels. You may also see a few ground squirrels if you live in the West or even chipmunks in warmer sections of the East.

The elaborate measures bird-feeding suburbanites take to rid their feeders of squirrels have given rise to a number of ingenious inventions, most of which purport to keep raiding squirrels away from the food supplies and none of which really works all of the time. Tree squirrels are acrobatic, clever, and thoroughly determined, and when their small minds are programmed to find a way to get bird food, as they often are, there is no device, it seems, that can keep them away. Better to increase your bird food supply and become a squirrel watcher.

One other mammal that may appear at your feeder is even less welcome than the squirrel. One winter I looked out the kitchen window and saw a long-tailed creature with a handsome brown coat nosing around in the snow beneath the feeder. I tapped the window and it was gone in a flash—a full-grown city-style rat. Unfortunately, he retreated not to the nearby shrubs and stone walls but to my cellar. I tolerated him for a month or so, and then when I counted no fewer than three rats (or four—I never could separate them exactly), I drove them out of the cellar with poison. One got its revenge by dying in the walls and stinking up the place for a week.

Since the feeder is a constant supply of food, not unlike a grain field when it is ripe, and since it will attract in its season most of the above seed-eating mammals, in keeping with good ecological law, you may spot from time to time a predatory mammal at your bird feeder. I have never seen one, but I have heard that people in more remote suburbs have seen red foxes stalking the snow below the feeder for meadow voles; and even in urban areas, there have been reports of weasels taking advantage of the presence of the voles. Furthermore, there is one other common predator in suburban areas that will indiscriminately destroy rats, mice, voles, and songbirds. Local cats, perhaps even your own, will spend an inordinate amount of time beneath or near the bird feeder waiting for whatever prey passes within their range.

Things That the Cat Brings In

If you keep a cat, periodically (in any season but winter) you may find on your back doorstep a forlorn mangled bit of brown fur that no more than half an hour earlier, perhaps, was a living creature. Many cats have a tendency to bring home whole mice, dead but uneaten, as if to repay you for all the cat food you have given them over the course of their lives. These gifts are sometimes left by the back door, and sometimes, much to the horror of whomever keeps the kitchen clean, they are laid gently by the cat bowl.

One of the more common mammals brought in by cats is the meadow vole. It can be recognized by its small eyes, blunt nose, round ears, and short tail. The common eastern mole, for which the meadow vole is often mistaken, is about the same size, but its ears are not visible and its eyes are so small that they are difficult to locate. The short tail of the mole is hairless, whereas the tail of the meadow vole is furred.

Some morning you may find what appears to be a baby mole on your doorstep, a tiny tube of fur with a very sharp nose and small eyes. If you look at the animal closely, you will see two sharpened front teeth that may have a red tinge to them. What you have probably found

LATE FALL

Short-tailed Shrew

is not a baby mole but a shrew, one of the more interesting mammals that inhabits the suburban wilderness. Shrews are the smallest mammals in existence, yet they are feisty predators and will take on, fight, and eventually eat almost any potential meal, including larger creatures, such as the meadow vole. They are very speedy, very aggressive, and, furthermore, have a toxic bite that can cause irritation in even so large a mammal as a human being and can paralyze and kill smaller mammals, such as mice. Even in death, the shrew may seek revenge. It secretes a substance that makes it unpalatable to predators, and although it may be killed, it often goes uneaten. This may be one of the reasons shrews are left whole on the doorstep by your cat. In spite of the nasty reputations, shrews are attentive guardians of the garden. They will consume many times their weight in insects each day.

If you live in a wooded area, the cat may deposit a deer mouse on your doorstep. This, along with the meadow vole, is one the most common gifts that cats proffer. On the other hand, some morning you may find a woodland or a meadow jumping mouse, a creature that looks very like a deer mouse but has an inordinately long tail and kangaroolike hind legs. You will not find either of these mice after October, nor before

LATE FALL

April. Along with the woodchuck and some species of bats, they are the only animals in the East that regularly hibernate in winter. By the end of September, the mice retreat to a grass- and leaf-lined nest well below the frost line. They will curl in a tight ball, wrap their long tails around themselves, and sleep through till May, living off a heavy layer of fat that is built up during the late summer of the previous year.

WINTER

THERE WILL COME a day or morning in early winter when the little projects in the yard and the last cleanup jobs in the garden are all rendered pointless. On this particular morning the ground will be covered with snow, and the world of your yard—the garden paths, the flower beds, the driveways, and the rock gardens—will be buried and made homogeneous by a smooth covering of white. The quietude of these mornings, the emptiness of life, is especially apparent after a night snowstorm. Step outside on such a morning and there is a high stillness to the air, a certain icy-bright desolation that permeates everything. It is more or less traditional to assume that this abrupt change in the landscape, this total submersion in snow, marks the end of the exploration of life in the back yard. Life outdoors from this point onward—at least in snowy regions—is now measured by good sledding hills or ski trails on the brighter side and, on the darker side, by trapped cars, endless snow shoveling, slippery walks, and discomfort.

Nevertheless, if you stay out for any length of time the morning after a snow and explore the confines of your yard, you will find that life goes on, even after the worst blizzards. Here and there after the first heavy snow, a few weed stalks may pierce the snow pack, and at the base of these lonely remnants of summer you may see a scattering of seeds and little bits of detritus. Look more closely at the base and you may see the tracks of birds in the snow. You may even see the birds themselves—juncos or field sparrows perhaps, flying from patch to patch, working over the seed heads and then moving on. The bird feeder will be crowded on such mornings, as cardinals, brilliant yellow and black evening grosbeaks, goldfinches in their olive winter plumage, field sparrows, bluejays, chickadees, and titmice flutter from the feeder to the bushes. Wait another day and then return in the morning to some of the more isolated sections of the yard, and you will see criss-crossing the landscape the tracks of mammals: the dotted line of deer mice making an ambling trail from one sheltering tree to the next, the pattern of rabbit tracks perhaps, squirrel tracks, or even the tracks of a possum or a raccoon.

In some ways, specifically because life is so sparse, you can observe more in this season than you can in others. Tracks, for example, will reveal the comings and goings of small mammals that you may never see in the flesh and whose presence would be unknown or go undiscovered in a warmer season. The bare stem of a goldenrod, the appearance of a winter moth, a scattering of snow fleas on any of the other insects and arthropods that are active in winter take on monumental significance. Except for the migratory birds, everything that was in your yard in summer can be found there in winter too, only in a different form. The annual flowers are now seeds, the perennials and biennials are rootstocks and tubers, the mammals are either hibernating or in dormancy, and the larger plants, the trees and shrubs, although stripped of their leaves and flowers, are no less interesting or alive.

It takes a certain amount of effort and organization,

but it is certainly worth making a point of periodically checking your back yard after heavy snowfalls. If necessary, you can shovel a nature trail around the property, taking in the various points of interest—larger trees, for example, weed stalks above the snow, or even obvious denning areas of mammals, if you are lucky enough to spot any. In any case, don't give up on winter. It can, admittedly, seem an interminable season in northern regions; but as will be abundantly clear by mid–April, winter is merely an interlude.

Trees

Even though they will all return by mid–May, there are not a lot of plants to be observed in your yard once the winter snows have covered all the grasses, weeds, and smaller shrubs. But, unless you live in the prairie regions or in one of those tract developments on former farmland that has been thoroughly stripped of native vegetation, there are often a number of trees in the average suburban back yard, any one of which may house an entire ecosystem. Theoretically, armed with enough guide books, and a sharp eye, you could spend the whole winter exploring the life cycles of the various species of vertebrates and invertebrates that exist in and on an older tree.

The trees themselves may present something of a challenge to the average back-yard naturalist during the winter. Without their cloaks of easily diagnosed leaves, the difference between a red oak and a black oak, for example, or a red maple and a sugar maple, can present something of a dilemma. Fortunately, you don't need leaves to identify a tree species, and since winter is a sparse season for plants, you can take your time identifying the various species in your back yard. Basically, identifying trees (or any living thing for that matter) involves a process of elimination. You learn certain characteristics of a species or a group, and if the tree you are attempting to key out doesn't fit the pattern, you exclude it and continue on until you have found what you are looking for. The branching habits of common back-yard trees is a good example. Twigs and branches of trees grow either alternately or opposite each other. Maples, ashes, dogwoods, and horse chestnuts have branches that are opposite, so if you notice that the tree you are trying to identify has branches that occur alternately, you know you are not dealing with a maple, for example.

Except for the ornamental species that are not necessarily native to the region, for the most part the trees in your yard will be the same as those in the nearby woods. If you learn the general species that grow in your area you can narrow down the choices; you will probably not have tulip trees in your yard, for example, or sourgums, if you live north of Connecticut. Once you separate the more obvious characteristics, you can begin observing the finer details. The bark patterns of trees vary from species to species, and if you learn some of the basic field marks, you can identify a species at a glance without ever looking up. Sometimes little anecdotes or catch phrases can help you remember the key characteristics. Gilly Robinson, my mentor in natural matters in my youth, always used to tell his charges that witches would come out each night and iron flat the rounded ridges of the butternut bark. He also used to tell us to watch for the "ski trails"—the white running lines high up on the trunks of the older black oaks.

If the bark can't help you identify the trees in your yard, the twigs might. The buds of each tree vary, and some have such a definitive appearance about them that

Shagbark Hickory

one glance will tell you the name of the tree you are looking at. Furthermore, on each twig there is a rounded or oblong pattern known as the leaf scar. This is the sealed "wound" that marks the place where the stem of last summer's leaf was attached to the twig. Each species has a characteristic pattern. In fact, some of the patterns resemble animals—a horse's face or a sheep's head. Once you learn to recognize this in the leaf scars, the identity of the tree will never be forgotten. Once again, Gilly Robinson has forever embedded his folklore in my mind in these matters. He would take us out to find the most evil tree in the forest. After a vain search (until we learned to remember the species), he would take us to a bitter-nut hickory. There, clearly marked in the leaf scar, he would point out the face of none other than Adolf Hitler—his hideous brush mustache showing clearly in the lower half of the heart-shaped scar. Nature all made sense as Gilly presented it to us. It was only natural that the face of Hitler would appear in a scraggly tree with a bitter, inedible nut that even the pigs reject.

Finally, if all else fails and you are unable to identify the species of tree by the bark or the twigs or the branching habit, you can take the easy way out and wait till summer when the leaves appear. After that, there can be no more excuses.

Winter Quarters

While you are attempting to identify the trees in your back yard, you might also watch for the many other living things that make use of the tree as a home base during the winter season. The tree is, in its own way, a marvelous plant, a sort of island community that provides all of the necessities of life throughout the year—shelter and nourishment in summer and protective hibernation or nursery sites during the winter. Some of these things seem so obvious that they hardly need comment. Squirrels eat acorns, obviously; and gypsy moth caterpillars feed on oak leaves. But beyond these simple facts, there is a complex dynamic of getting and spending, of effects and counter-effects, reverberations and interconnections. As my friend Megan Lewis used to say about gardening, "All is interplay."

White Ash and Keys

One example of this complex interrelationship of the tree and the things that feed on it may serve to alert you to interactions in your yard. Trees often fruit in cycles—heavy one year, light another. The ash trees bear a plentiful crop, it is likely that a large number of the fruits or keys will remain on the trees well into January, after the migratory winter finches arrive from the north. Pine grosbeaks, evening grosbeaks, redpolls, and siskins are fond of ash fruits, and in a good year these birds will descend on a tree during the day and pick over the remaining fruits. Many of the uneaten keys will become dislodged in the process and fall to the ground, and at night deer mice may emerge to feed on the leavings.

You can observe this cycle if you happen to have ash trees in your back yard. Watch the trees during the day for flights of birds, and on the morning of the following day, if the snow conditions are right, look on the ground around the bottom of the tree. In all probability, you will see many little split keys lying about and the tracks of mice lacing the trunk of the tree like a wreath.

You may also notice, if you live in an area that has any woods nearby, a little story in the snow—a tragedy of sorts, if you happen to be partial to mice. If you follow your mouse tracks carefully, you might see that the trail of some innocent individual emerges from a sheltered spot, dawdles among the fallen ash keys for a while, and then seemingly disappears as if the mouse had somehow taken flight. In fact, the poor mouse may have taken flight—its first and last—in the talons of an owl. If you look around the tracks of the disappeared mouse and the snow conditions are very good—i.e., a windless night and a fresh light snow cover—you may be able to see the wing tracks of the owl. They will look like two brush strokes on either side of the place in which the mouse had its last meal. In some cases you may notice a drop or two of mouse blood.

Bark Life

Often in winter, deep in the crevices of the bark of the older trees, you can find an elongated brownish beetle with two pink shieldlike appendages on the side of its head. For those who have spent any time hunting the summer fields for fireflies, this should be an easily identified insect; it looks exactly like the lightning bugs that you catch in your back lawn in summer and, in fact, is in the same family. The beetle that you find in the crevices of the bark in winter, however, is a lightless version of the summer cousins. It does not bear the light-making equipment.

These little insects often proved very useful to me back in the days when I took people out on field trips. It is of course common knowledge that insects die or disappear in winter. Children are well aware of that fact, and adults seem even more secure in their knowledge of insect life cycles. Invariably, on some trip in the winter woods, I would bring up the subject of insects in winter; and after I had been assured by the attendees that all the insects were either dead or lying dormant as eggs or pupae, I would bet that I could find a living insect within five minutes. Even in areas I was not familiar with, I could always locate the lightning bug beetles on the south side of some oak or hickory. (I should point out that I would never wager on bitterly cold overcast days; they seem to disappear on such days.)

Beneath the Bark

Life goes on inside the tree as well as in the branches and the bark. If you have any dead trees on your property, unless they are a direct threat to your roof, you might consider letting them stand. A dying or dead tree with its easily excavated trunk interior and its host of insects tends to attract a high number of nesting birds, such as woodpeckers and chickadees. These cavities may be further excavated by squirrels and then finally may be lived in by raccoons or possums (pp. 256–60). But apart from these more obvious inhabitants, there is, beneath the exterior covering of the tree, a whole host of insects, feeding, pupating, mating, and birthing.

Most of these insects are boring beetles, which feed on the host plant and then burrow into the wood to lay eggs. The beetle that inhabits a given tree on your property will vary from tree species to tree species. If you have a sugar maple on your property, you can expect to find the sugar maple borer—or signs of it anyway, somewhere on the tree; or you may be able to see signs of the round-backed apple borers on your apple trees. But although the borer species may vary from tree to tree, the technique for laying the egg follows the same general pattern and can be observed beneath the loose bark of old trees of any species.

Generally the adult female boring beetle lays her eggs on the bark of the tree in question and the newly hatched larvae bite their way through the thick bark to spend the winter pupating in the snug nurseries beneath it or just inside the sapwood of the tree. The life cycle of the engraver beetle is typical of these species. The adult female drills or eats her way through the bark and drills out a tunnel or groove in the wood below it or in the bark itself. She lays her eggs in this groove, and after the larvae hatch, they dig their own tunnels out from the egg groove, pupate, and then emerge as adults by chewing through the layer of bark. If you lift the bark of an old or dead tree, you can often see the remains of these nurseries. They look like carved out centipedes—a long groove with radiating legs on either side. You may also be able to see in many trees the tiny holes known as shot holes, which the adults of some species of boring beetles have dug in order to escape or lay their eggs.

You may also find beneath the loose bark of dead trees the pupae of insects such as the gypsy moth, as well as hibernating spiders and beetles. The egg sacks of certain species of spiders may also be placed beneath loose strips of bark during the summer or fall. Typical of these is

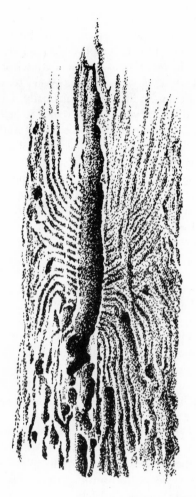

Engraver Beetle Nursery

the egg case of the grasss spider. It is about an inch or so in diameter and consists of a convex mass of white silk that is almost viscous and will stretch itself interminably, it seems, if you pull on it—very tough in spite of its delicate appearance. When it finally does become dislodged—that is, if you are determined to pull it apart—it will come off in little tufts, like bits of fluffy cotton. Inside this silky covering is another layer of material that serves to protect the eggs.

Finally, on a number of occasions, peeping under loose bark, I have often come across the disorganized jumble of grasses, feathers, odd pieces of cloth, and the like that make up the next of the ubiquitous deer mouse. They seem to occupy any available nook and cranny in the world.

There is another bark beetle that you might be able to observe in cut or split wood, although it is hard to spot under the bark of standing trees. You may notice in a sawed-off tree stump or in the split log a long, black, threadlike channel that branches and has a cluster of shorter tunnels at the end of the lines. These are the tunnels of ambrosia beetles, an insect that bores straight into the center of the tree rather than along the surface, as do the other boring beetles. The clusters are the nurseries. Once the young hatch, the adults feed them on a fungus grown by the adults in the longer tunnels and then pushed into the nursery tunnels to be consumed. Although the ambrosia beetles seem to have a preference for apple trees, this primitive form of farming may be going on in your own back yard, even if you don't have any apple trees. It is believed that when the beetles move to a new species of tree, they carry the spores of the fungi with them in order to start new "farms." Watch for the tunnels in the stumps of any trees you have cut down on your property or in the logs in your woodpile.

You may also notice after you split open a log a little knot of what appears to be dead ants. These are undoubtedly dormant carpenter ants who were living in a colony in the tree when it was cut down. Unlike termites, carpenter ants do not eat wood; they simply burrow in trees, fence posts, and sometimes buildings in order to construct their living quarters. The nest consists of a series of interconnected galleries and chambers part of which you will be able to see inside the split-open log. You may also see carpenter ants in your house during the warmer months, and if you are unlucky, you may even have them living inside the timbers. In general, however, carpenter ants seek out wood that is in contact with soil, so if your foundation is clear and your house timbers are above the ground, you probably don't have to worry if you see a few carpenter ants in your kitchen.

Gypsy Moths

You may also see on the bark a fuzzy yellowish mound about two inches long—the egg case of the gypsy moth. Much to the dismay of the suburban landholder, come spring these eggs will hatch and the tiny caterpillars will emerge to feed on the leaves of the surrounding trees. Gypsy moths, like many living things, are cyclical. Some years there are none or few, and in other years they will devastate thousands of acres of forest and suburban land. In time, as with most natural populations, either viral or bacterial diseases or predator populations will blossom along with the increased numbers of gypsy moths, and the cycle will crash and things will even out.

The general opinion now among environmentalists is

that the natural forest can withstand one or two infestations of gypsy moths. In fact, some foresters believe that the overall health of the forest may improve, since the weaker individual trees will be weeded out by the caterpillar, leaving more room for the healthier trees. That does not say much for the appearance of your grounds during the all too brief summer season, however. It does seem unfair to wait six or eight months for the appearance of the green verdure of your yard only to have it cruelly stripped away in late June. As you may know if you have endured a gypsy moth infestation, the leaves will come back by August, but that does not make June any better.

There are a number of home cures that you can employ around your land without resorting to dangerous pesticides. One of these is to scrape away all the egg cases during the winter months and dispose of them. You might get in the habit of removing the egg cases while you are looking for more benign creatures. The system doesn't always work in years of serious infestations, since the caterpillars can migrate to your property from nearby areas, but generally you can keep things under a certain amount of control if the outbreak isn't at a zenith in your region.

I don't know whether this has any significance or not, but there was a bad infestation in my area of New England a few years ago. In contrast to my neighbors, who spent an inordinate amount of time plucking off egg cases, painting trees to stop the ascent of the caterpillars, setting out traps, and finally, when all else failed, spraying their trees with toxic chemicals, I did nothing. When the caterpillars finally blossomed, in spite of the fact that I had oaks and wisteria on my land—favorite food plants for gypsy moths—and in spite of the fact that I did nothing to control them, the caterpillars seemed to welcome the challenge of my neighbors' control programs and spent most of their energies consuming their ornamental trees, leaving my oaks and wisteria alone.

Bark Birds

Gypsy moth egg cases are large and easily spotted; but hidden in the crevices of the bark, wrapped around the smaller twigs or lined out along the branches, or anywhere on the tree for that matter are the egg cases and pupae of the insect populations that depend on the tree for survival. Once you begin to notice these tiny signs of life, you will see them almost everywhere you look. This may be of mere passing interest to all but the most serious student of entomology, but to the various species of insect-eating birds that remain in the north during the winter, the insects are the very essence of survival; their presence is the difference between life and death. If you watch the trunk of a tree for any length of time during a winter day, unless you live in an area that is relatively treeless, at some point one of the bird species that depend on these insects will probably appear.

One of the most common and also the most colorful of these is the nuthatch. Nuthatches eat both insect and plant material, whichever is most available or in season. They are common visitors at the bird feeder, but you may also notice that they will spend time carefully running down the trunk of the tree from which your feeder is suspended. It is interesting to me that toward the end of winter, after who knows how many inspections, by who knows how many different nuthatches, the birds always seem to find something to eat in the crevices of the bark of the tree nearest my feeder. Furthermore, they never seem to tire of the search, even though a plentiful supply of food is located no more than a few yards away at the feeder.

The nuthatch generally goes about its business upside down; it will begin at the top of a tree trunk and work its way down. By contrast, the brown creeper, which also depends on tree trunks for survival, will begin its search at the bottom of the trunk and work its way up, spiraling each tree as it ascends. This is one of the least conspicuous birds in the forests of the American continent. It is small, and it is patterned and colored very much like tree bark. If it were to remain still, it would be difficult to spot. Fortunately for the bird observer it seems to be in near constant motion, spiraling up one trunk, flying to the next tree to repeat the process, and so on until it disappears from sight. Creepers do not feed on plant food, but like a number of unrelated species of winter birds, they sometimes seek out bird company, so that from time to time during the winter one may appear at the tree near your feeder. Generally, though, these birds are best seen by luck. One way to locate them is to listen for their high-pitched squeaky call note; it is to my mind a fairly distinctive bird sound. I often hear creepers before I see them.

Seed-eating chickadees and titmice also spend a certain amount of time searching the trunks of trees for those few morsels the nuthatches and the creepers overlook. But perhaps the most typical bark-dependent bird in your yard is the woodpecker. There are some twenty-three species of woodpeckers in North America. Some of these, such as the arctic three-toed and the pileated, are relatively rare or uncommon throughout most of suburban America; but others, such as the hairy woodpecker, the downy, the red-headed, and the red-bellied, are found nearly everywhere. The downy woodpecker and its larger relative, the hairy woodpecker, feed on wood-boring beetle larvae, as well as bark-dwelling bugs, such as scale insects and beetle moths and ants. Both species are found throughout the United States and are among the first birds to take advantage of suet set out at a bird feeder. Like the nuthatches, they may come originally to feed on offerings set out by benign human beings, but almost out of habit, it seems, they will hunt food on trees near the feeder.

In the South and Midwest, the red-bellied woodpecker and the red-headed woodpecker may be as common in your yard as the hairy and the downy. They, too, tend to assiduously work over the trunk of trees in your property and the surrounding neighborhood, even in urban areas. Both of these species tend to feed on more plant food than the downy and the hairy woodpeckers. The red-bellied will eat nuts, fruits, and berries along with its diet of beetles, grasshoppers, crickets, and ants; and the red-headed woodpecker feeds on plant material, such as cherries, as well as beetles and other insects.

Woodpeckers have a fairly distinctive whinnylike call that, although it varies from species to species, has a sort of woodpeckerness to it that is unmistakable. If you live in a region that is fairly heavily wooded, and you are lucky, you may hear on some day in late winter a rather louder woodpecker whinny, a call that sounds, in the words of one child I know, like the call of a flying horse. If you are luckier still, you may see a great dark bird the size of a crow fly through your yard with a peculiar dipping flight. The pileated woodpecker, although rarer than any of the other common suburban woodpeckers, does manage to survive in the midst of human company. If you have any around your property, they will make their presence known at some point, not so much by their calls but by the peculiar damage they do to the trunk of vulnerable trees. If you see a large oblong or rectangular hole in one of your trees, you will know by the size and the distinct squared shape of the diggings that you have a pileated nearby. The hole is really quite a dramatic affair; no other species, save perhaps for little boys with axes, could inflict such damage to a tree trunk. The holes are excavated in order to dig out carpenter ants, one of the favored food of the pileated. Do not begrudge this beautiful woodpecker its handiwork; the ants will do more damage to the tree than the holes. In any case, more often than not the tree they tear apart is half-dead anyway.

If you have fruit trees in your yard, you may notice during your winter inspection a series of lines of perfectly executed holes running horizontally around the trunk. This is the work of the yellow-bellied sapsucker, a species that is found in the East, Midwest, and Far West. The bird drills the holes, allows the sap to drip out, and then drinks it. The sap may attract a number of insects, which become trapped and will be eaten by other birds, such as warblers, chickadees, and creepers. In some cases, the sap from the trees may ferment before the sapsucker returns to drink, and there are reports—although I'm not sure I believe them—of drunken birds cascading around orchards and well-landscaped back yards.

Given the industrious nature of woodpeckers, and the contingent of chickadees, nuthatches, and titmice with whom they often assemble, and furthermore given the numbers of these birds and the amount of time they spend in the yards of people who feed them, one would suspect that by feeding birds in winter, you could be fairly well assured that the tree-dwelling insect population of your property would be diminished. Since a lot of the

insects that depend on trees are pest species for orchard-
ists and property owners—if not for forest ecosystems—the birds should be welcome guests. As it is,
however, insect populations such as gypsy moths have
a seemingly unceasing resilience—they make it back every
year in spite of the birds.

The Ecology of the Woodpile

The life inside or on a tree does not necessarily come to
an end simply because the tree is chopped down, cut
into lengths, and split. If you have a stack of firewood
on your land that sits for any more than a few months,
you may notice as you take it apart to use it that it contains in its nooks bits of stored grass, a stash of seeds
here and there, a daddy longlegs or two, and an assortment of seemingly unidentifiable beetles. The woodpile
on my property, in spite of the fact that it is heavily
used, offers one of the most regular contacts with the
natural world that I experience during the winter months.
Every day, it seems, I make some little discovery there.

I have noticed over the years that there seems to be a
dynamism to the life that exists in the woodpile. It is to
my mind a significant and highly metaphorical ecosystem, since by its very nature it is doomed. The wood
that you bring to the woodpile will already have inside
it many species of boring beetles and other pupating or
adult insects. Once stacked, however, this imported
community will begin to change. One of the reasons
dead trees attract so much wildlife to them is that they
offer shelter. And what is true of the tree is true also of
its parts; as a result, beetles, spiders, insects, centipedes,
and other invertebrate that appreciates the shelter of bark
will seek out the woodpile. Furthermore, higher ani-

mals may be attracted by the nooks and crannies that are created by the stacked wood. Every year I find shed skins of garter snakes in my woodpile, and down at the base of the stack or sometimes below the pile I find a redback salamander and a contingent of sowbugs, centipedes, wireworms, click beetles, fireflies, and millipedes. And without fail, each year, as you might expect, I find at least one deer mouse nest, sometimes containing the young pinkies, as the baby mice are called.

It occurred to me a few years ago that the woodpile, not unlike your bird feeder, has all the elements of the living communities that operate in large ecosystems. It has its predators, in the form of the spiders, some of the beetles, and the salamanders and the snakes. It has its prey—the consumers, in the form of the boring beetles and the mice; and it has its decomposers, in the form of millipedes, sowbugs, fungi, and bacteria. It also has its seed stashes, or middens, its nurseries, its eggs, and pupae, and all the potential to continue on forever—with, of course, a little input of outside energy from the world beyond the woodpile. But the interesting thing about this particular ecosystem is the fact that it is so transitory, so totally dependent upon the exigencies of human behavior. Sometime in the late summer or fall, the householder builds the woodpile; but no sooner has it been set up than he or she proceeds to slowly take it apart. By the end of winter, any woodpile worth its weight will have been fed into the fire. One hopes, of course, that we do not see here a metaphor for the ecosystems of the whole planet; and yet there are, it seems, some ominous similarities.

Wintering Insects

The eggs and pupal sacks of wintering insects are not confined to the bark or inner bark of standing trees. If

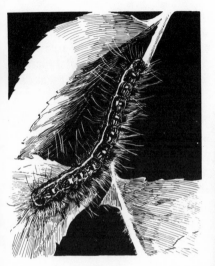

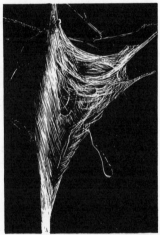

Tent Caterpillar Nest

you search your yard carefully, you can find a wide assortment of shapes, colors, and style concepts—a sort of Parisian spring of fashions just above the snows of your own back yard. Look especially on the outer twigs of trees, on the stems of shrubs above the snow, and on any grasses or weed stems that remain above the snow. Almost any tree, for example, will have at least a few egg cases of the fall cankerworm, an insect that can sometimes be a serious pest on fruit and shade trees. The egg cases look like tiny flower pots; look for them especially on elm and apple trees. You may also see, suspended from a twig or plant stem, a curious mass of tiny sticks, pine needles, or old leaves. This is the egg case of the aptly named bagworm, which can also be a pest to conifers; if you happen to find a large number of these on your property, it might be a good idea to pluck them off.

On black cherry or apple trees you may see the eggs of the tent caterpillars. They look like a ring or ball wrapped around a twig. The eggs will hatch in the spring and the larvae will feed on the leaves of the trees. They construct a weblike tent around the twigs and outer branches which, if torn apart with a stick, will be found to contain a squirming mass of hairy caterpillars with brilliant blue spots running down their backs. You might also find around your yard a holster-shaped egg case of the pistol case-bearer moth, or the elongated case of the cigar-case bearer. Both of these appear often on fruit trees.

In contrast to some of the above pest species, you might also find a yellowish clump with ribbed sides attached to the stems of a weed stalk or pasted up against the house wall or the wall of an outbuilding. If you do see such an egg case, leave it alone; it probably contains the eggs of thousands of future praying mantises, one of the better-known pest controllers of the home garden (see page 147). Horticultural supply houses often sell praying mantis egg cases to greenhouse keepers and gardeners as an alternative to pesticides. The emergence of the tiny praying mantises, which are exact replicas of the larger adults, is one of the small spectacles of nature that can be observed in the wilderness of the garden. As one acute observer commented, the young mantises stream out of the egg case with all the hope and determination of workers released from a factory on the Friday before a long weekend. I'm not sure that it is an analogy one would want to carry too far. If they are confined, the predatory instincts take over and the young mantises will begin to eat each other.

Finally, if you live in an area that has no snow, or if you experience a snowless season, you may be able to find a few hibernating adult insects around your yard. Houseflies, wasps, cluster flies, and mosquitoes may hibernate inside your very house or in the walls of garages or outbuildings. Hornets and yellow-jackets may hole up in damp, weedy areas along stone walls or wood edges, along with adult ground beetles, weevils, leafhoppers, lady bugs, and other species. Inside a rotting log you may find adult wireworm beetles, click beetles, fireflies, and creatures such as millipedes, centipedes, spiders, and harvestmen. You may also find a number of vertebrates, although the mere act of discovering them may end their reign forever on your property. If you have any rotting wood on your land and you want to chance destruction, you can dig into it in winter and you may find hibernating wood frogs, a snail or two, or even a red-backed salamander. By tearing off the protecting layer of soft wood, you will allow the entry of cold air, and no matter how carefully you reconstruct to hibernaculum, you may have undone the frogs or salamanders. Since these animals are cold-blooded, they are torpid during the cool weather and generally are not able to burrow deeply into the wood on their own. It might be better, given the reality of the situation, to imagine that each rotting log on your property is rife with beneficial species such as frogs and salamanders. Look for them in warmer weather if you must.

Galls

Those not entirely familiar with trees may, after carefully studying the twigs, bark, buds, or leaves, be thor-

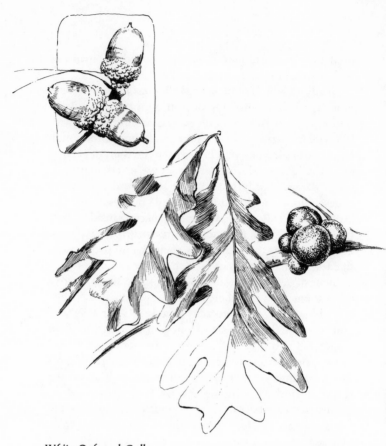

White Oak and Gall

oughly thrown by the fruit that appears on some oak trees in winter. You may notice, even if you can recognize oaks at a distance, that some of the branches bear on their twigs small clusters of round objects slightly larger than an acorn. These are oak apple galls, a growth created by the tree at the insistence of a gall wasp larva. Sometime in the summer, the adult gall wasp laid an egg on the twig. Once the egg hatched, the larva drilled into the twig and released a substance that caused rapid cell division, thus creating the gall or fruitlike object you see on your oak trees. If you can reach the cluster of galls (they sometimes live in groups) and cut one open carefully, you may be able to spot the small grub dwelling inside its chemically induced winter quarters. On the other hand, if you notice a small hole in the gall, in all probability the gall is old and the adult has long since hatched and emerged into the world.

Don't worry if you can't find an oak gall. If you look carefully around your yard in winter and you have a variety of plants, you will probably be able to find a gall of some kind or another. The creation of plant galls is not an uncommon survival technique among insects, and although there are variations on the theme, basically the galls are manufactured in the same fashion. The larva of the insect burrows toward the living cells of the plant and secretes a substance that stimulates growth. As the gall develops, the larvae of many species feed on the tissue and at the same time continue to release the chemical that causes the growth. Not a bad system, really, for survival in the ruthless tooth-and-fang world in which most insects exist. The gall provides both food and shelter, somewhat like a benign, nourishing gingerbread house.

As is often the case in the natural world, however, no sooner does a good system evolve than something else will come along (after a few million years of evolution) and undermine it. In the case of the gall insects, any number of insects who are themselves incapable of creating galls learned over time to break into the gall houses and set up living quarters there. Many of these species are harmless inquilines or guests that do not necessarily harm the gall maker. Others, however, parasitize them. Furthermore, there are parasites that prey only on the guests and leave the makers alone, as well as parasites that feed on both the gall creators and the guests. So many species of insects may rely on the gall for survival at some point in their life cycle that it is difficult to determine who made what and who is living where. The pine-cone gall, for example—which, as its name implies, looks a little like a tiny pine cone—may have as many as thirty-one different species of gall makers, guests, parasites, and transients depending upon it. Evolution, in case you haven't noticed, is alive and well in your own back yard.

Watch for galls on oak trees, on willows, on goldenrod stems, on raspberry stems, and, as many gardeners know, on rose stems. Some of these galls may be inconspicuous little dots or swellings; others are elaborate hairy, spongy, or fuzzy things.

Summer in January

Sometime around the middle of January there may be an abrupt rise in the temperature. Fog and mist will drift above the snow, the sun will seem to take on a warmth that is reminiscent of March or late February, and if it continues for more than a few days, you may be lulled into believing that you have gotten through yet another

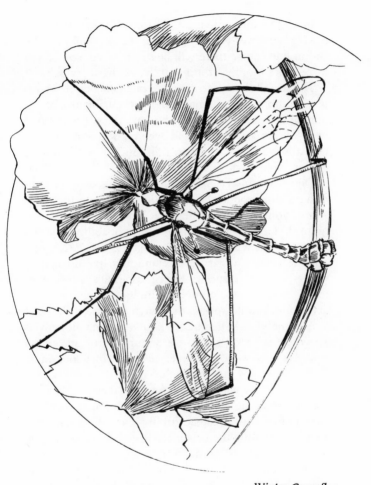

Winter Cranefly

winter. The interlude is all illusion. Within a few days the temperatures will drop again, the sky will go cold, and in due course there will be snow—two, sometimes three more months of it if you live in the snow belt.

The so-called January thaw is a phenomenon that takes place almost every winter, and the inhabitants of the human community are not the only ones that respond to it. Mammals, insects, and even on occasion amphibians are fooled by the warm air. It is a good time to explore your back yard.

One of the insects you may notice outside your windowpane or around the warm outer walls on the south side of your house is a thing that looks like a large mosquito. In fact it is a crane fly—in all probability a species known as the winter crane fly, which is active throughout the year. The larvae of crane flies live in shallow waters, and some species emerge as adults in mid-winter. There are also a number of midges, as well as a few genuine mosquito species that hatch in winter.

A somewhat larger insect known as the stonefly is active in winter. There are a number of species of stoneflies you might encounter; generally they look more like cockroaches than flies—dull-colored creatures with long bodies and wings held flat against their backs. They are slow-moving and easy to catch, although they will attempt to run away rather than fly if you disturb them—again, very unflylike behavior. If you don't see any in your yard and you want to have a look at one, take a winter walk along a running brook some warm winter day. They are very common and often bask on rocks and tree trunks, near streams.

One species of crane fly or snow fly that emerges during the winter does not have wings; in fact, it looks more like a spider than a fly. You can sometimes see them walking over snow during the January thaw, and they are commonly seen later in the winter as the weather begins to warm. They emerge usually on sunny days and mate above ground, but the female will burrow or crawl beneath the snow after mating to lay her eggs in the leaf litter at the base of trees.

You may also see snow fleas on top of the snow. A curious phenomenon used to occur at one of the nature centers where I worked. Every February, about the middle of the month in a rite of winter, people would begin calling to ask us to identify a strange form of pepper that appeared generally at the base of a rock or tree. It looked exactly like grains of pepper, with one significant difference—these black grains had the alarming habit of periodically springing into the air.

The tiny specks of life, we would patiently explain, were snow fleas, a primitive form on insect that belongs to the genus *Collembola*. Oddly enough, snow fleas are found not only on snow in back yards and nearby woodlands but in tidepools. They are very easy to recognize; there are very few insects abroad during the snowy days of mid-winter, for one thing, and for another, very few insects are so evident, even in summer. Snow fleas have the habit of clustering together in herds of thousands, so that whereas one might be easily missed, the herd as a whole is hard *not* to see.

Snow fleas jump into the air by flipping a springlike appendage on the thorax—the hind end of any insect. The reason for this apparent escape mechanism is not entirely clear, since the snow flea does not appear to be a major food source for any predator. Some species in the snow flea family do not have the appendage. Watch for snow fleas on sunny days at the base of trees. They feed on plant material such as algae and fungi and sometimes appear in great numbers around maple sugaring buckets.

WINTER

Honeybees

Another insect you may see during the January thaw symbolizes, in the minds of many, the very essence of summer. The mere association of bees and flowers brings to mind hot afternoons and the languor of the summer garden. And yet, during the uniquely warm days of January, bees often emerge from their hives and fly around for a while. At times you can see individual bees on tree trunks or vegetation above the snow and on the outside walls of your house. I have found them crawling across snow on warm days, and invariably I find them—often dead, I am sorry to say—on the ice of a nearby lake where I skate in winter. Sometimes individuals become imbedded by the quirky weather conditions—a thaw, followed by a hard freeze.

Unlike most insects, bees remain active throughout the winter inside the hive. As soon as the outside temperature falls below 57 degrees, bees will begin to cluster, forming a large ball. The bees in the center of the ball feed on the honey stored in the comb, and as a result of the metabolic process generate heat, while those unfortunates on the outside serve as living insulation. This cluster of life will expand or contract depending on the outside temperature, and periodically the entire ball will switch positions so that those on the inside become the insulating layer and those on the outside move in to eat. Since they are inside the hive all winter and are, in effect, eating throughout the winter, waste inside the hive could theoretically create unsanitary conditions over a period of months. But bees are notoriously clean insects, forever scouring the hive, removing detritus, waste, and foreign matter—they even have a squad of maids whose sole duty is to maintain sanitary conditions. In order not to foul their own nest, whenever the weather is warm enough, bees will emerge from the hive to defecate—a so-called cleansing flight. If you keep bees, or if you happen to be near a hive on a warm day in winter, you can often get a good view of the activity. You may also see the yellow dots of the bee droppings on the side of the white hives and on the snow in front of it.

LATE WINTER

IN ANY PART of the country seasons tend to merge, spring has elements of winter, winter has elements of fall or spring, and summer has days when a chilly night or a clear, breezy day brings on all the feelings generally associated with autumn. This merger of seasons should come as no surprise; after all, the clear demarcation of the natural year into four strict seasons with definitive beginnings and endings is an invention of the human mind. Except for the celestial events (which we human animals have chosen as markers for seasonal changes), there is no real difference in the natural world between one week in late winter and another in early spring. The progression toward summer is a continuum; you cannot simply say today is winter and tomorrow will be spring.

One of the clearest examples of this is late winter, a season that seems to have all the elements of full winter—snow, sleet, bitterly cold days, high winds, and notorious winter storms. And yet as early as February, if you become alert to the subtle changes that operate throughout any season, you can sense the beginning of the end of winter. You have but to listen to the bird calls around you and watch the progress of the buds on the wild shrubs and trees. Late winter is also the mating season for many species of mammals. Foxes, skunks, and raccoons begin courting around mid-February in many sections of the country, and if you have even a few acres of undeveloped land around you, or for that matter even a few good den trees or burrows, you will hear the squabbling that goes on.

Late winter is the season of sleet, to be sure, but it is also the season of maple sap. It is the season of snow, but it is also a season of dull stirrings in the thawing earth. It is the season of the thickest ice, and it is also the season in which the ice breaks up and the migratory ducks return. It is the season of snow storms, but it is also the season in which the first snowdrops appear. And of all the myriad little events that take place in the back yard in late winter, there is probably none as welcome or as well known as this modest blossoming. It says somehow all there is to be said about hope and rebirth, and yet the event may take place as much as a month before the beginning of official spring.

Running Sap

Long before the first of spring you may be able to glimpse a preview of the coming season. On some of the trees in your yard or along the roadside, you may notice little icicles hanging from the ends of twigs. These will probably appear sometime in February during a period when the temperatures creep above freezing during the day and then dip below 32 degrees at night. The classic indicator tree, and the one most famous for its sap, is the sugar maple—which is not solely a resident of New England and Canada, as many believe, but ranges south

Sugar Maple

to Georgia and even Texas. A sugar maple is not easy to recognize in winter unless you know the general shape of the tree and the texture of the bark. If you have any doubts, check for vertical grooves in the trunk and the ridged dark brown bark. The twigs are shiny and the buds of the tree are pointed, a little like tiny awls. The frozen icicles of sap at the ends of the branches are not necessarily diagnostic, since the sap is running in many trees at this time of year, but if you live in the proper region, since sugar maple is a common tree you might check for the other identifying details.

If you have a sugar maple in your yard—even if you have only one—it might be worth your while to tap it some year to make maple syrup. Even if you don't get around to the syrup-making end, you can treat yourself to a little fresh raw sap. It tastes like the cleanest, sweetest spring water available, perhaps better. Before drinking, unless you are not squeamish, it might be wise to strain the sap through a sieve. It is surprising how much debris, including gnats and flies, will collect in an uncovered bucket.

There are entire books devoted to the art of home maple sugaring, so I needn't burden you with the details. Suffice to say that it is an interesting though time-consuming hobby, best performed in an outdoor evaporator. I have heard too many stories about wallpaper steamed off the walls because someone attempted to boil down sap over the kitchen stove. It takes forty gallons of sap to get a gallon of syrup, and the rest of the liquid ends up as steam.

Sugar maple is not the only tree with drinkable sap; black birch also has a sweet-tasting sap that can be boiled down into a wintergreen-flavored syrup. One of the easiest ways to identify the black birch in winter is to eat it. The twigs are black and have little white spots on them, and if you break one off and chew it, you will get a taste of wintergreen. The black cherry also has spotted twigs, but it has a flavor or smell of almond if you break the twig (the taste is decidedly bitter, however). I have never made a syrup from the birch, but I have tasted the sap, and it has the delightful spring-water-pure taste of sugar maple, spiced with an elegant but subtle flavor of wintergreen.

If you want a similar flavor without going to the trouble of tapping the tree, you can collect a handful of the twigs, break them or cut them in small pieces, and steep them in boiling water for five minutes or so. You can also make a good birch beer from the twigs. Simply collect a few bundles, break them up, stir in honey and birch sap, and follow the general direction for making any beer. My friend Hatch Griggs, who is an avid wild-food addict, used to make birch beer early in the spring and serve it up at his annual May Day feasts. In good sap years (or beer years), his festivals would often end in failure. Everyone would get too tipsy to enjoy the subtle tastes of the wild repasts he was famous for. This birch beer is no relation to the mild drink that is sold in country grocery stores—it's the real thing.

Mammals

Apart from the fact that snow acts as an insulating blanket protecting roots of plants from deep frosts, and apart from the fact that meadow mice and shrews may be safe from predatory owls and hawks in their subsnow tunnels and runways, the presence of snow offers the average back-yard explorer a means of deciphering some of the action that takes place in any given back yard under the cover of night. Once a good base of snow is established, no mammal can cross your yard without your knowledge. Wherever they go, terrestrial beings that are active in winter will leave tracks, and through these you can get a better understanding of some of the things that are happening around your property when you aren't looking.

There are any number of good guide books to tracking, as well as a lot of posters and charts you can hang up on your refrigerator door. (Most of these will include species such as bobcats and weasels, which will rarely be seen in your yard). It is fairly easy to learn to identify the few common mammals that will come to your yard during the winter months. Rabbits, squirrels, voles, mice, chipmunks, skunks, and raccoons are the most obvious ones to study first. And after a morning or two outside after a fresh snowfall, you should be able to pick up a few tricks of the tracking trade and in a short period of time learn to identify the species that are regularly using your yard.

This, however, is only the beginning. Once you have learned the alphabet of tracks, you can begin to read the words. And in time, you will find that you can read whole stories there. The deer mouse/owl tale recounted on page 222 is a case in point. But there are many such stories—squirrels that descend trees, venture out into the snowy ground, and then change their minds; rabbits that rise on their hind legs to nip buds, lose their balance, and topple to the ground; and similar little bits of daily life.

The stories do not end with the tracks, however. Be sure to watch for other signs in your yard of mammal activity: chewed bark and branches, droppings, scattered seeds, gnawed twigs, holes dug in the snow, seed caches, and similar signs often turn up at the end of an animal trail.

Cottontail Rabbit Tracks (right)
Gray Squirrel Tracks (left)

LATE WINTER

Flying Squirrels

There is one mammal whose track may elude you no matter what the season. Flying squirrels do not set foot on earth as often as their cousins, and furthermore, although they do not hibernate, they tend to hole up longer during the winter months, especially if the weather is bad. Nevertheless, if you have a well-supplied bird feeder and have maintained it for a number of years, and if you have trees or forest nearby, it is entirely possible that you may have a regular population of flying squirrels on your property. These squirrels are nocturnal, so the only way to find out if you have them is to set up an outdoor light near your feeder. They may be wary at first, but if the squirrels are eating regularly, they will become accustomed soon enough and drift in for a meal in spite of the lights.

Flying squirrels do not really fly. They are merely excellent gliders, climbing up tree trunks to gain altitude and then drifting from trunk to trunk. If you are lucky enough to see one during the day, you will notice that they have flattened tails and a flap of loose skin on either side of their bodies. When they jump, they spread their legs and soar with an easy arcing flight that is to my mind as beautiful as that of soaring birds. At the end of the flight, just before they land, they dip slightly and arrive head up on the bark of the tree with a seemingly airy, almost ethereal elegance.

Flying squirrels usually set up quarters in an old woodpecker hole. Their nests are lined with bits of shredded bark and other plant material. They feed on nuts and seeds, like other squirrels, but they will also eat birds eggs and they occasionally will eat the baby bird itself, a seemingly ruthless practice for so delicate a creature.

Flying Squirrel

I learned to find flying squirrels during the day from my friend Carolina, who is an irrepressible nut gatherer and craftswoman. She used to spend a lot of time in the forest during the nut season in fall, and invariably she would carry with her a light stick. Whenever she would come to a tree with a woodpecker hole, she would beat on the trunk and holler for the flying squirrels to come out. Nine of every ten trees she would hammer on would be squirrelless, but at some point during her forays, the small head and bright eyes of a flying squirrel would appear at the hole and glare at the intruder. I have beaten on any number of trees in the years since I met Carolina, but only once or twice have the squirrels appeared. It is an art, perhaps, that has been fully developed only by nut gatherers and basket weavers like Carolina, but it's worth a try in your yard if you happen to have any good woodpecker holes.

LATE WINTER

Some time ago I lived in a house in which flying squirrels became something of a problem. The place was heated—if you could call it that—by a kerosene stove fitted into the chimney of an overly large fireplace. Each fall as heating season approached I would hear rustling in the old kerosene stove. It was something of a problem disassembling the stove to get at the noise, but it was worth the effort. On every occasion I would find an innocent flying squirrel covered with soot trapped inside the fire box. Evidently it would have come down or fallen down the chimney, seeking winter refuge. I'm sorry to say that virtually each one of these seemingly gentle squirrels attempted to bite me even as I set them free. No matter, I came to admire their spunk.

Possums

One of the tracks you may see around your bird feeder in the morning after a light snow is a peculiar, almost deformed-looking foot with a toe or thumb that is decidedly askew, pointing inward or even backward as if it had been broken. The track is that of a possum, a common visitor to bird feeders, garbage cans, and compost heaps. Possums, in the view of the general public, do not rank among the most beautiful animals in North America. You will not see images of them on animal greeting cards, and to my knowledge, although there are any number of bears, raccoons, squirrels, kangaroos, and the like in the average child's stuffed animal collection, there are no stuffed possums. Possums look a little like large rats; they have pointed noses and long, naked tails. However, their fur is gray and their ears are large and hairless and generally black in color. If you approach one it will crouch, hiss, feign death, and, when all else fails, release a foul-smelling greenish substance from a gland beneath its tail. This survival technique—total surrender as opposed to flight or fight—seems to have worked well for the possum; it is the most ancient mammal in North America, having endured on this planet some sixty million years. It is also the only North American marsupial. The young are born early in the spring after a gestation period of less than two weeks. They are tiny pink things, no bigger than a large bumble bee, but they have an unerring sense of direction and, as soon as they are born, clamor to the mother possum's pouch and attach themselves to a nipple. There they will remain for the next two or three months, venturing out to ride on the mother's back after two months or so.

I am somewhat fond of possums. I like to see them nosing through the compost heap in the late summer light, I like their ghostly whitish images, which often appear in the headlights along the back roads in rural areas, and I like the bright, beady eyes. And I also like the idea or the philosophy that the possum lives by—its nonviolent retiring behavior. The fact that the possum is such a successful mammal. raises to my mind some serious questions about the nature of intelligence. The general theory is that possums are small-brained, stupid creatures with a limited world-view; yet they have survived glaciers, continental drifts, periods of drought, periods of volcanism, and any number of similar changes in the world ecosystem, whereas more intelligent creatures, such as humans, may be in the process of obliterating their own life support system. Who is to judge which is the more intelligent creature?

The possum's ability to survive is evidenced not only by the fact that it is spreading northward into colder regions but also by its ability to survive in suburban and even urban areas. It was a common inhabitant of the suburban town in which I grew up, and I have heard of possums in cities throughout the southeast and mid-Atlantic states. The possum will eat almost anything, including other mammals, such as mice. It regularly feeds on frogs, fruits, snakes, worms, insects, and of course garbage. They tame fairly easily if you want to set food out for them, and unlike skunks, they do not start fights in the spring and will not spray your dog or cats. If you want to risk attracting skunks and raccoons to your property, you might set out a dish of cat food for your local possum.

Raccoons

Many of the North American Indians felt a special affinity for the bear; the animal was held sacred in some groups and figures heavily in the folklore of almost all the tribes in areas where both bears and people live. Part of this attraction may have something to do with the bear's footprint. Like the track of the human being, it is plantigrade, or flat-footed, and so the Indians may have assumed that it was in some way closer to them than other animals of the forest. In fact, in the language of one southern tribe, the word for bear is "man of the woods."

You probably won't see any bears in your back yard, certainly not beneath your bird feeder, but at some point you may see a track that is in effect a smaller version of the plantigrade footprint of bears and human beings. Raccoons have long toes on both the front and hind paws, and true to plantigrade form, you can see the full foot in the track. Generally the raccoon places its hind foot next to its front foot as it moves from place to place. Watch for the tracks around your compost heap and beneath your bird feeder late in the winter when raccoons became more active.

Like the possum, this is one of the mammals that has done well in suburbia, a sort of upwardly mobile creature that seems to adapt well to the changing environment. They are common garbage thieves and, in fact, can be something of a pest in some areas. Raccoons have very agile front paws; they are able to manipulate small objects and can even learn to open locked cages. This same ability is put to use during night raids on garbage cans. They can undo all but the most tightly secured lids, it seems, and they are, furthermore, very messy eaters, fond of shredding wrapping papers into small bits and spreading garbage can contents throughout the yard. If you see a particularly devastating attack on your garbage, it is probably the work of raccoons; possums are far more gentlemanly about their feeding customs, in spite of their primitive heritage.

Generally in the wild raccoons feed on other animals; mice, bird eggs, baby birds, grasshoppers, and the like figure heavily in their natural diet. But they are also somewhat aquatic in their habits. They are good swimmers and regularly hunt frogs, crayfish, and fresh-water mussels. The little bit of folklore about raccoons washing their food probably developed because of their feeding techniques. They use their sensitive front paws while hunting for aquatic food, feeling along the bottom of shallow bodies of water with a washing, wringing motion. They also tend to dunk their food in water if there is a stream or pond near the food supply, but the habit has nothing to do with cleanliness. It is believed that the dunking makes the food easier for the raccoon to swallow. They will also eat vegetation such as berries and nuts, but true to their adaptable form, they are notorious corn feeders. Reportedly raccoons will wait all summer for the corn in your garden to reach just the right stage of ripeness. Then when it is ready, in a single night they will move in and devastate your patch. Techniques for keeping the raccoons out of corn vary from place to place. Some people leave radios playing all night in the garden as the corn begins to ripen, and one woman I know, who for years suffered serious losses, finally left a note for the raccoons, pleading with them not to steal her crop that year. She claims the technique worked that one year only. One thing is clear, killing them doesn't seem to do any good. The farmer behind my house trapped 120 raccoons over a one-year period and still lost his corn—sweet vengeance, I suppose. Since you can't beat them, you might as well join them; I always plant a little extra corn and assume that I am going to take some losses.

Unlike the possum, raccoons are commonly featured on posters, cards, and as a substitute for teddy bears. They have a prominent black mask, a banded bushy tail, and a decidedly pointed nose. The mask suggests some kind of cosmic order that we mere mortals have yet to understand—they are, as I say, notorious thieves.

Meadow Voles

Mammalogists have estimated that the meadow vole, or meadow mouse, may be the most common mammal in the United States. Meadow voles live at ground level in the grass-roots jungle of open areas such as fields and lawns. They are extremely prolific, capable of producing about thirteen litters per year with four to eight young in each litter; theoretically, one female could produce 100 voles in a single year. Fortunately, predators such as

Meadow Vole

weasels, hawks, owls, and foxes serve to keep them under control.

The meadow vole's life is circumscribed by grass. It travels through its world by a system of burrows or tunnels that it makes just at ground level under the stems of long grasses and under the mat of dead grass that appears in all but the most thoroughly manicured lawns. If you have even a few square yards of unmowed or untended grass at the edge of your property, or if you did not get around to mowing your grass at the end of the growing season, you can expect meadow voles. Vole nests consist of a ball of grasses and twigs and are located just above the ground and below the mat of grass. The only occupied nest I have ever found was turned up by my dog, a companion, who for all her faults has a way of assisting in many of the little discoveries I have made in the various yards I have had. If you do happen to find a meadow vole, you might easily mistake it for a mole. It is about seven inches long, has a short, stubby tail, a rather large head with a blunt nose, and tiny glistening slits for eyes. The cat, if you have one, may lay a few at your back door from time to time; they are slow-moving and easy to catch. Moles, by contrast, have sharp noses and no eyes at all (see page 212). Late winter is the best time to look for meadow voles. After the snow melts, or after the winter grasses have matted down, you can easily see the outline of their runways. The number of these always impresses me; they criss-cross fields and lawns like tracks in a rail yard.

Spring in February

There is another sign of spring that takes place fairly early in the winter—sometimes as early as January in southern regions. There are a number of bird species that, although they may not nest until spring, begin singing their courtship songs and staking out territories in wintertime. Several of these species are in fact associated with the South, but in recent decades there has been a general drift northward of southerly species and some of these species are now found as far north as Vermont and Minnesota and into Canada. Typical of these is the brilliantly colored cardinal, easily one of the more spectacular North American birds. Cardinals have a beautiful call as well as a beautiful plumage. The song is a clear whistle that slowly descends with an eloquent subtlety and ends with a sharp "chip" or "tsip" as a sort of coda. Cardinals will appear at your feeder in the winter—one of the common visitors—but it is not until February that they come into their own as songbirds. Their song could have spelled their end at one point.

Before laws were passed prohibiting such acts, cardinals used to be kept as cage birds.

Another whistler that begins singing in February is also associated with the South. The tufted titmouse—which seems to have moved north at about the same general pace as the cardinal—has a clear whistled call similar to the cardinal's. As the field guides describe it, the cardinal sings "what cheer, what cheer, what cheer" in a descending pattern, whereas the titmouse repeats the words "peter, peter, peter" again and again. Neither of these descriptions, of course, can summon up the feeling associated with these beautiful songs. A touch of warmth in the wind, melting snow, the drip of icicles, or rain, infused with the call of cardinals and titmice, is more or less the essence of late February.

Chickadees also begin singing about this time of year. Throughout the winter, you will undoubtedly have heard their call note, which is their name repeated over and over again. But in February, the chickadee will begin to whistle the word "phoebe" repeatedly. This is such a clean enunciation of the word "phoebe" that one of the first mistakes of novice bird watchers is to believe that the phoebes have returned when the call sounds out from the shrubbery in February. In fact, the phoebes will not return until March or April, and when they do, they will *say* their name; the chickadee sings it.

Chickadees and titmice are tame birds. When they are busy at the feeder, if you move slowly enough you can get within a few feet of them, and if you exhibit a certain amount of patience and don't mind standing in the cold, you can get them to eat from your hand. No matter how experienced you are at bird watching, no matter how many birds you have studied through binoculars, there is something very interesting about observing these common birds close up. The subtle beauty of the feathers, the bright eyes, the nervous habits, and the seeming intelligence of these birds always impress me when I get a good close-up view of them. One wonders what dull, birdly concept they form about the upright creatures that proffer food to them.

Cardinals, titmice, and chickadees are the prominent voices of February. But late in the month other birds will start singing. The song sparrow begins to court in late winter, the long warbling song of the purple finch may be heard high in the tree tops, and the first returning migrants may appear. Listen for the familiar "onk-a-ree" call of the red-winged blackbirds and the clear whistle of fox sparrows. The season of bird song always reminds me of a Mahler symphony. It begins quietly enough in early February, adds voices by March, brings up the cellos and the woodwinds by April, and by mid-May has the full orchestra crashing about the forest even before the sun is over the horizon.

A little later in the season you can hear all of these songs from the throat of a single bird. While they have a wonderfully languorous song of their own, mockingbirds are excellent mimics and are one of the common residents of suburban back yards except in far northern areas. They will begin singing as early as January or February in the South and somewhat later in the season—by mid-March, for example—in New England. I remember distinctly one year hearing a phoebe call in early March long before the phoebes generally arrive in the area where I live. I was suspicious, of course, since there are mockingbirds around my land, so I searched out the call and found a mocker singing an absolutely perfect rendition of the phoebe song; all that was missing was the phoebe. In all probability, the mocker had been moving north with the phoebes and had pulled ahead of the pack, so to speak. I once heard in the same general area a mockingbird with a phenomenal repertoire. He would start with a resounding bluejay call, sing as a mockingbird for a while, then render the song of the cardinal—perfect pitch—then a tufted titmouse, then a phoebe, then the phoebelike call of the chickadee, a mocker again, a bluejay again, a perfect robin song, a short medley that seemed to include a starling's chattering, a red-winged blackbird, and then a mocker again as finale. My friend Megan Lewis, a gardener, once told me she was overjoyed when mockingbirds finally extended their range to her land in New England. "They fill in the empty spaces in the spring bird chorales," she used to say.

Great horned Owl

The great horned owl is one of the more spectacular birds of the wooded areas of Canada and the United States. It is a mysterious bird—large, secretive, night-flying, and associated in the minds of poets and myth-makers with death, superior intelligence, and any number of similarly anthropomorphic qualities. The bird is also, in the minds of many, associated with wild land, deep forests, and inaccessible ravines. Great horned owls are found in such places, but not surprisngly, given the spread of suburbia in recent years and the natural adaptability of this owl, they can be found in suburban areas as well.

Although I'm sure there is no relation between the two facts, it is curious that the great horned owl is one of the few animals that commonly feeds on another suburban survivor, the skunk. One of the ways to identify the presence of a great horned owl nest is the decidedly skunky smell that permeates the area around the nest if the owl has recently fed on some unsuspecting skunk.

The skunk is a small part of the great horned owl's diet; generally they feed on birds such as grouse, mice, and other small mammals.

The nest of this owl is often located on top of an old crow's nest or squirrel's nest, often in a pine tree. It is a great bulky affair constructed from sticks thrown together in a seemingly random pattern. You don't have to go tramping through the nearby woodlots, however, in hopes of finding the nest of the great horned owl; there is an easier way to tell if there is one in your neighborhood. Great horned owls nest in February, and as is often the case in the bird and mammal world, the rituals surrounding courtship and mating involve a certain amount of noise. If you hear what sounds like a huge dog barking in the distance some night in February, listen again; it may be a great horned owl. The call or song consists of five or six deep hoots, which, unlike the barking of a dog, will be repeated in a regular pattern: five or six barks followed by silence, then five or six more, and so on—sometimes for an hour or more. There is a patch of woods behind my house, and each February, around the twelfth of the month, great horned owls start waking me up at night. It is a great relief to me to hear them calling—a little like the call of the spring peepers.

There is one other way to find owls, and in this case, in my experience at least, it is one of the few opportunities you may get to see the great horned owl during the day. Crows seem to have a natural aversion to owls. This may be because owls occasionally take birds as food, possibly crows, and the crows are simply protecting their territory. But whatever the reason, if a flock of crows discovers an owl, the birds will assemble their forces and begin diving on the owl, cawing loudly. The agitated calling seems to attract other crows in the area, and unless the owl makes good its escape, a huge flock of angry crows may gather. If some morning in any season of the year you hear a lot of crows, you might investigate. As you approach, the flock may seem like nothing more than an idle congress of crows, but come closer and you will see a large, thick-winged, thick-bodied bird—usually just a silhouette—fly out, followed by the excited crows.

Springtime in the House

The change of light in late winter and the warming days do not go unnoticed in the hibernating insect community, and perhaps nowhere is this reawakening more apparent than in your house. If you live in an older house, unless you are a diligent housekeeper you may have a few colonies of spiders and insects sharing the walls of your home. I am not speaking here of unwanted pests

Paper Wasp

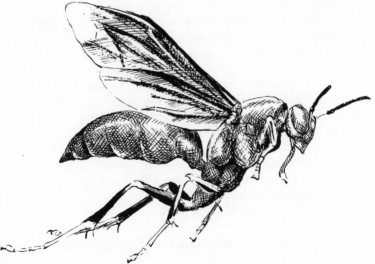

such as cockroaches, ants, and silverfish but of less commonly observed species such as wasps and jumping spiders.

I have a preference for older houses myself and in fact never lived in a place that didn't have its share of polistes wasps, or paper wasps. These benign creatures mate in the fall and after mating crawl to protected areas to spend the winter. In many cases they will seek out the warm walls of human dwellings, and unless you clean them out somehow they will be there come spring. The warm days of late winter seem to bring them to life; you can see them crawling around your windowpanes toward the end of February. Sometimes by late spring they can become pests.

The insects that you see during winter are all female. Both males and females hibernate in the fall, but for whatever reason, the males do not live through the season. The gravid females become fully active in mid-spring and begin to construct paper cells in which they will lay their eggs. In two weeks the eggs will hatch and the queen will feed them until they pupate, about two weeks later. The adults that emerge will form the work force that helps to build the summer colonies.

The nest of the paper wasp may often be seen on the side of your house; it consists of a collection of papery gray tubes or cells attached to the house by a spindle. Paper wasps are slow to sting, and the sting itself isn't all that powerful. Furthermore, the males are sluggish creatures with no stinging capabilities—you can pick them up and handle them at your leisure if you are so inclined. With a little practice, you can learn to identify the sexes— females have dark faces and the males have yellow faces and decurved antennae. A notoriously bad boy in the neighborhood where I grew up somewhere along the line obtained this little bit of information and used it to

Jumping Spider

get back at his enemies. He would announce that *anyone* can handle paper wasps and with total indifference would reach onto a hive, pluck off a male, and then challenge his enemy to do the same. After a certain amount of taunting, the innocent victim would reach for the hive, inevitably pick up a female, and get stung in the process. I am sorry to say that those of us that were privy to the information never released the secret of the trick to the initiate until after he or she was stung.

There is a small, harmless spider that may also appear in your window frame during sunny days in late February. Jumping spiders seem to have a preference for human habitations. Part of this attraction may be due to the fact that they prefer a dry, warm habitat, and the south-facing window of a heated house meets all the requirements. Unlike many arachnids, these aptly named spiders catch their prey by leaping upon it. They are sprightly little animals, often brightly colored, and they move with a jerky attentiveness. They are capable of greater leaps comparatively, than gazelles or kangaroos, and they seem to be able to go sideways, backwards, or forwards with equal ability.

You may also begin to see house flies in late winter. Most flies winter over as larva, but adults sometimes winter over in warm niches if they can find any, and since your house offers many such sites, there may be a few sluggish individuals here and there around the windowpane. Unlike the summer flies, they are slow at this time of year and easy to swat. In some sections of the country, the flies may appear in hordes. These are probably cluster flies, a species closely related to the house fly. They often winter over in the walls of older houses in large numbers and emerge as the weather warms in spring.

Wood Frogs

One of the common telephone inquiries nature centers receive is a question about a small brownish frog with a black mask that the caller has found in the cellar of the house. During the autumn, wood frogs, like other amphibians, seek out hibernation spots or hibernacula, and since suburban houses may be in its territory, this frog takes advantage of adversity and seeks out the damp, frost-free cellar to spend the winter. You will be likely to find them there during damp weather in fall and again in spring.

Wood Frog

LATE WINTER

There is another way to tell whether you have wood frogs in your neighborhood. Some warm day as early as February in some regions, you may hear what sounds like a group of contented ducks quacking in the woodlot across the street from your house. Unless you know what it is, the noise offers an odd challenge to the curious naturalist. Approach the sound and it will cease altogether, only to start up after you leave. The woods or empty lot from which the sound emanates may have a shallow body of standing water, nothing more than a puddle in some cases, and clearly nothing that would serve a duck. If you sit down by the side of the bank of the temporary pool and remain silent for a few minutes, the sound will start up again, and if you look carefully, floating in the middle of the water, legs extended, you will see the same frog you may have found in your cellar in autumn. Wood frogs are generally the first frogs to start calling in the spring, beating, sometimes by a few weeks, the famous bellweather of the season, the spring peeper.

Eggs are laid in the pond after a short mating period, and following mating the adults will disperse to the surrounding woods. The gelatinous masses of wood frog eggs may contain as many as 2,000 eggs, and the whole jellylike mass may be attached to a submerged stick or log. The eggs may freeze if there is a cold spell following mating, and in some cases the shallow ponds wood frogs seem to prefer may dry up early in the season. But in spite of the seemingly high mortality rates, generally the wood frogs are successful breeders, common throughout their range. Once the water warms sufficiently, the eggs will hatch and the tadpoles will spend the next six to eight weeks in the pond feeding primarily on tiny aquatic life that shares the body of water, including other wood frogs.

Wood frogs look like amphibian raccoons. They are

dark brown to a rich, reddish brown or even a coppery tan and have, as I mentioned, a distinctive black mask, extending from the snout past the eyes to the back of the head—really one of the more handsome frogs in all the forest. They are excellent jumpers and very well camouflaged in their normal habitat. If you surprise one in the woods, it will leap off with athletic zigzagging jumps that may cover as much as five feet per leap. They are very difficult to catch.

Mourning Cloak Butterflies

Once the snow has melted back and the forest floor is clear, the progression of spring seems to speed up considerably. One of the first signs of this increased activity may be the appearance of an insect normally associated with hot summer gardens and meadows—namely, the butterfly. Unlike many butterflies, which commonly winter over as pupae or eggs, the adult mourning cloak goes into hibernation in autumn. It will seek out a sheltered spot beneath bark or under a dry log or rock, fold its wings, and go into a torpor for the season. During warm days late in the winter, sometimes as early as February even in the northeast, the mourning cloak will take off and flutter through the forestlands. If you live in a wooded region, you can often see them on the south side of your house on warm days in late winter. They are among the most subtly beautiful of all the butterflies—rich brown velvety wings tipped with yellow stripes, dotted with flecks of blue.

After mating, the female mourning cloak lays her eggs on poplar, willow, or elm trees, and in a good year for these butterflies, the caterpillars may strip the leaves of your favorite ornamental, thus creating yet another moral dilemma. Do you kill the caterpillars of this beautiful butterfly, or do you allow your favorite tree to appear dead for a few months? I leave the decision to you, but the tree will set new leaves by mid-summer.

Mourning cloak butterflies are common throughout the United States and Canada. They belong to a group of butterflies known as the angle wings, named for the notched, angular forewings that insects in this group possess. Many species of angle wings hibernate in winter, and although in my experience none emerges as early as the mourning cloak or is as common, you can sometimes see other species flying through your yard in late winter.

Mourning Cloak Butterfly

Wetlands

If your house happens to have been constructed in or near a former wetland, you may notice that in some sections of your property or in a nearby woodlot a body of water will appear each winter shortly after the snow begins to melt. These areas of standing water may last no more than a month or two; by summer they will be indistinguishable from the surrounding woodlands. But short-lived though they may be, these temporary pools or ponds have their own ecology. A number of insects, plants, and amphibians have adapted themselves to their short life spans.

Skunk Cabbage

Often the ponds have characteristic vegetation around them, and of this perhaps the most interesting, the wild version of snowdrops, so to speak, is the aptly named skunk cabbage. The spearlike tip of the spathe containing the flowers of this plant may appear in February, in some cases before the snow is off the ground. Usually you can see the tips of the plant poking up through sphagnum moss or moist soil on the edges of the temporary pool. Once the flowers have pushed up out of the ground, you can see the purplish spathe surrounding the true flowers. This is often the only plant blooming when the bees emerge from their hives during warmer days in late winter, and if the conditions are right, you may spot not only bees but a number of other pollen-dependent insects around the plant. As the weather warms in the spring, the leaves will follow the flowers and develop fairly quickly into rounded, cabbagelike bunches that grow to about three feet. The plant gets the name from the odor of the flowers. If you so much as brush

Skunk Cabbage

the flower, it will give off a strong musky scent vaguely reminiscent of a skunk.

Hellebore

The leaves of the skunk cabbage are edible, and reportedly some Indian groups would make use of the rootstocks as well. But growing next to skunk cabbage is a plant known as hellebore, which is one of the most toxic leafy plants in the northeast. Hellebore first appears as a rather attractive, green, elliptical spear that looks lush and edible. Shortly after its appearance, if the growing conditions are right, the plant will put up a fine display of handsome shiny leaves. Unlike skunk cabbage, whose leaves grow in a clumped, cabbagelike bunch, hellebore's leaves grow out from a single upright stem that may reach seven or eight feet in height. The leaves have killed cows and horses who have grazed on the young shoots and may cause death in human beings. Apparently hellebore doesn't taste very good, however, and it is rarely implicated in poisonings.

Wetland Shrubs

Growing near the temporary pond, or in your own back yard perhaps, you may see the black alder, or more properly, the winterberry holly, which has red berries that often stay on the shrub well into winter, and the spice bush, which has handsome dapple twigs that have a unique spicy taste. You may also notice some trees that typically grow in wet areas. Red maple, which ranges from Newfoundland south all the way to Florida, is one of the more common of these. It is the tree that turns New England a flaming red in autumn, and in spring it puts out a wealth of dark red flowers that, when mixed with the subtle hues of a rainy April day, cause swamps and wet areas to stand out like torches in an otherwise colorless landscape. American elm, black ash, black gum tupelo, and many species of willows also grow near temporary ponds.

Fairy Shrimp

Wood frogs are not the only living things that make use of these short-lived wetlands. Some species of salamanders and toads and a number of invertebrates, such as whirligig beetles, may also be seen in the clear waters, although the amphibians generally appear somewhat later in the spring. Of the invertebrates, perhaps the most thoroughly adapted to the temporary life-stye that is required by existence in these bodies of water is the fairy shrimp. This curious animal, which is only vaguely related to the shrimp, mates in the later winter as the ice breaks up from the small forest pools—generally about the same time the wood frogs begin calling. They are notoriously unpredictable about their populations. A pool on or near your land may have thousands one year and none the next, but it is worth looking for them in any case. They are about an inch long, very shrimplike, and they almost always swim on their backs, propelling themselves by means of tiny oars or leaflike legs. Their bodies are translucent; you can see through to the innards—heart, digestive tract, and red blood. Fairy shrimp require cold water to survive, and after mating, after the eggs are laid and the waters of the temporary pools begin to warm in the spring sun, the adults begin to die. By summer, the puddle that appeared in your yard may be no different from any other part of your land, but buried in the soil, even if the sod dries out completely, are the living eggs. They will winter over and then hatch in the following spring.

Second Spring

Not long after the skunk cabbage goes into leaf, after the wood frogs begin calling and the fairy shrimp and the mourning cloaks appear, the sun will cross the line in the sky known as the ecliptic, and spring will officially begin.

One of the things you will notice if you stick with your back-yard studies for more than a year is that the natural world operates according to a fairly strict schedule. If you keep a record of the natural events that occur in your yard it will become clear that the birds return, the grass turns green on the lawn, and the flowers blossom at about the same date each year, give or take a few days. And here, it seems to me, is one of the underlying messages of nature study and one of the things that accounts for the continuing interest in the outdoors in an age that is decidedly technological in its orientation. Although it is obviously a very real and essential aspect of existence, nature is also an excellent metaphor for order. No matter how chaotic and disordered daily life or world politics may seem, given half a chance, and with complete indifference to human events, the migratory birds will return, the frogs will call from the swamps, and the flowers will blossom in their appointed season.

INDEX

281

INDEX

INDEX

INDEX

INDEX

INDEX

INDEX